# HAWAII TRAVEL GUIDE 2025

A Comprehensive Travel Companion To Explore Hawaii And Everything You Need To Know

**CRYSTAL RICHARD**

# Copyright © 2025 by Crystal Richard

All rights reserved. No part of this publication may be reproduced, distributed, or transmitted in any form or by any means, including photocopying, recording, or other electronic or mechanical methods, without the prior written permission of the publisher, except in the case of brief quotations embodied in critical reviews and certain other noncommercial uses permitted by copyright law. For permission requests, write to the publisher at the address below.

## Table Of Contents

**INTRODUCTION TO HAWAII**.....................9
**MAP OF HAWAII**..............................................14
**CHAPTER 1**.............................................................15
    Aloha Spirit: Understanding Hawaiian Culture.............................................................. 15
    Geography and Overview of the Hawaiian Islands............................................17
    Climate and Best Time to Visit Hawaii. 20

**CHAPTER 2: PLANNING YOUR TRIP**.......24
    Travel Requirements and Entry Information for Hawaii................................ 24
    Transportation: Flights, Ferries, and Local Transit in Hawaii..................................27
    Budgeting and Costs: What to Expect When Traveling to Hawaii........................... 31
    Sustainable Tourism: Responsible Travel Tips in Hawaii......................................................34

**CHAPTER 3: THE ISLANDS OF HAWAII.39**
    Oahu: The Gathering Place.........................39
    Maui: The Valley Isle.......................................42
    Big Island (Hawaii): The Orchid Isle....... 45
    Kauai: The Garden Isle.................................48

Lanai and Molokai: Off the Beaten Path... 52

**CHAPTER 4: MUST-SEE NATURAL WONDERS.................................................56**

Hawai'i Volcanoes National Park: A Natural Wonder................................. 56

Na Pali Coast: Kauai's Breathtaking Jewel........................................................ 59

Haleakalā National Park: Maui's Majestic Volcano.................................................62

Waimea Canyon: The Grand Canyon of the Pacific................................................ 66

Beaches and Bays: Best Spots for Sun and Sand in Hawaii......................... 69

**CHAPTER 5: CULTURAL AND HISTORICAL SITES........................................ 73**

Pearl Harbor and WWII History: A Crucial Chapter in Oahu.............................73

'Iolani Palace and Hawaiian Royal History: A Glimpse into the Monarchy...76

Pu'uhonua o Hōnaunau National Historical Park: A Sacred Sanctuary......79

Polynesian Cultural Center: A Celebration of Pacific Heritage................82

Native Hawaiian Traditions and Cultural

Experiences: A Living Legacy.................. 85

**CHAPTER 6: OUTDOOR ADVENTURES AND ACTIVITIES..............................................89**

Hiking Trails in Hawaii: From Easy to Extreme..................................................................89

Water Sports in Hawaii: Surfing, Snorkeling, and Diving..................................92

Whale Watching and Wildlife Tours in Hawaii: А Natural Spectacle......................95

Ziplining, ATV Tours, and Helicopter Rides.........................................................................99

Golfing in Paradise: Top Golf Courses in Hawaii............................................................ 102

**CHAPTER 7: BEST BEACHES OF HAWAII... 106**

Waikiki Beach: The Jewel of Oahu........ 106

Lanikai Beach: A Slice of Paradise on Oahu..................................................................109

Ka'anapali Beach: A Maui Gem.............. 112

Hapuna Beach: A Pristine Paradise on the Big Island.................................................115

Hanalei Bay: A Jewel of Kauai.................118

**CHAPTER 8: HAWAIIAN CUISINE AND DINING........................................................... 122**

Traditional Hawaiian Foods: Poi, Poke,

5 HAWAII TRAVEL GUIDE 2025

and More.......................................................... 122

Best Luau Experiences in Hawaii.......... 125

Farm-to-Table: Local and Sustainable Dining in Hawaii............................................ 128

Popular Local Eateries and Fine Dining in Hawaii...............................................................132

Farmers Markets and Food Trucks: A Taste of Local Flavor in Hawaii............... 136

## CHAPTER 9: ACCOMMODATIONS: WHERE TO STAY............................................................... 141

Luxury Resorts and Beachfront Hotels in Hawaii....................................................................141

Vacation Rentals and Boutique Inns in Hawaii............................................................... 145

Budget-Friendly Hostels and Camping in Hawaii............................................................... 149

Eco-Friendly Stays: Sustainable Accommodation Options in Hawaii..... 154

Family-Friendly Hotels and Resorts in Hawaii................................................................159

## CHAPTER 10: HAWAII'S NIGHTLIFE AND ENTERTAINMENT......................................... 165

Luau Shows and Live Performances in Hawaii................................................................165

Night Markets and Cultural Festivals in

Hawaii..................................................169

Bars, Nightclubs, and Beachfront Lounges in Hawaii......................... 174

Stargazing on the Big Island....................178

Sunset Cruises and Dinner Cruises in Hawaii..................................................182

## CHAPTER 11: PRACTICAL TRAVEL TIPS AND SAFETY..............................................187

Health and Safety in Hawaii: Ocean Safety and Sun Protection.........................187

Traveling Between Islands: Flights and Ferries in Hawaii............................................ 191

Packing Tips: What to Bring for Your Hawaii Vacation............................................. 196

Local Etiquette and Customs in Hawaii.... 200

Emergency Contacts and Traveler Resources in Hawaii.....................................204

## CONCLUSION: EMBRACE THE ALOHA SPIRIT IN YOUR HAWAIIAN ADVENTURE................................................. 209

8 HAWAII TRAVEL GUIDE 2025

# INTRODUCTION TO HAWAII

Aloha! Welcome to the Hawaii Travel Guide 2025, your gateway to discovering the wonders of these tropical islands. Hawaii is more than just a travel destination; it's a paradise that invites you to experience its warm spirit, natural beauty, and vibrant culture. Whether you're an adventurer, a nature lover, or someone looking for pure relaxation, Hawaii offers something for everyone. But before we dive into the details of this incredible destination, let me share with you a personal story from my own journey to Hawaii.

I vividly remember the first time I stepped foot in Hawaii. After a long flight, I arrived at Honolulu International Airport on the island of Oahu. The moment I walked off the plane, I was greeted by the warm tropical air, and a sense of excitement washed over me. The airport was bustling with people, many of them clad in flowered shirts and leis, symbolizing the famous

Aloha spirit that I had read so much about. Despite my exhaustion, I couldn't wait to see what Hawaii had in store for me.

I picked up my luggage and made my way to the rental car desk. As I drove away from the airport, I felt like I had been transported into a different world. The sun was setting, casting an orange and pink glow across the sky, and the smell of the ocean filled the air. My destination was Waikiki, a bustling beachfront area known for its iconic beach and vibrant nightlife. On my way there, I passed palm trees, towering volcanic mountains, and miles of coastline. Every turn seemed to reveal another breathtaking view, and I couldn't resist pulling over to snap a few photos of the scenery.

When I finally arrived at my hotel, I was greeted by the sound of traditional Hawaiian music playing softly in the background. The staff welcomed me with warm smiles and a refreshing glass of pineapple juice, and I immediately felt the island's hospitality. From my room, I had a spectacular view of the ocean, with Diamond Head in the distance. As I stood on the balcony, watching the waves crash onto the shore, I realized I had just begun to scratch the surface of this incredible place.

The next day, I woke up early and decided to explore the island. I started with a hike up Diamond Head, the iconic volcanic crater. The hike was challenging but rewarding. As I reached the summit, the panoramic view of Waikiki Beach and the vast Pacific Ocean was breathtaking. The combination of the bright turquoise waters, the lush green mountains, and the city below felt surreal.

After the hike, I spent the afternoon lounging on the soft sands of Waikiki Beach. The water was warm and clear, perfect for a relaxing swim. I even tried my hand at surfing for the first time. Though I wasn't particularly good at it, the thrill of catching my first wave was unforgettable. That evening, I attended a traditional Hawaiian luau. The smell of roasted pig filled the air, and I enjoyed the lively hula performances that told stories of Hawaii's rich cultural heritage. It was a magical night filled with delicious food, vibrant music, and the camaraderie of fellow travelers.

In the following days, I visited other parts of Oahu, including the historic Pearl Harbor, where I reflected on the significance of the site and its impact on world history. I also explored the lush rainforests and cascading waterfalls on the island's North Shore, known for its massive winter waves and laid-back surf culture. The more I experienced it, the more I fell in love with Hawaii.

My trip to Hawaii was a perfect blend of adventure, relaxation, and cultural immersion, and I knew it wouldn't be my last visit. The islands have a unique way of making you feel at home, even if you're thousands of miles away. Whether it's the natural beauty, the friendly locals, or the deep sense of history and culture, Hawaii has a magnetic charm that's impossible to resist.

This travel guide is designed to help you experience Hawaii as I did, by immersing yourself in everything it has to offer. From exploring its famous beaches to discovering hidden gems on its lesser-known islands, this guide will be your companion to making the most of your Hawaiian adventure. Aloha, and welcome to Hawaii!

# MAP OF HAWAII

**Scan the QR code to view the map of Hawaii**

**Note: While the map you see here gives you a broad overview of Hawaii, it won't pinpoint specific spots like hotels or eateries. But don't worry! If you scan the code right up there, it'll launch Google Maps on your gadget. Once you're there, you can easily plug in wherever you want to go and navigate the city like a pro. Thanks!**

# CHAPTER 1

## *Aloha Spirit: Understanding Hawaiian Culture*

The Aloha Spirit is much more than a friendly greeting in Hawaii. It embodies the essence of Hawaiian culture, a way of living that fosters kindness, respect, and love for others and the land. Rooted in ancient Hawaiian traditions, the word **"Aloha"** itself holds deep meaning, translating not just to **"hello"** or **"goodbye,"** but to **"love," "peace,"** and **"compassion."** It's a guiding principle for how people interact, connect, and live in harmony with the world around them.

Understanding the Aloha Spirit is key to truly appreciating Hawaiian culture. Central to this philosophy is the idea of ohana, which means **"family."** However, in Hawaiian culture, family extends beyond blood relations. It encompasses the broader community and even nature itself. Locals treat visitors as part of their ohana, often welcoming them with open arms and a warm sense of hospitality. Whether you're staying in someone's home or simply enjoying a conversation with a local, you're likely to feel the genuine warmth and friendliness that comes from this deep cultural value.

Another key concept linked to the Aloha Spirit is malama **'aina,** meaning to care for and respect the land. Hawaiians have a strong connection to nature, and the islands themselves are considered sacred. Traditionally, the land is not something to be owned but cared for, and this respect is reflected in their sustainable practices, such as fishing and farming. When visiting, you're encouraged to adopt this mindset, ensuring you leave the islands as beautiful as you found them. From avoiding single-use plastics to participating in beach clean-ups, being a responsible traveler is an important way to honor the Aloha Spirit.

Hawaiian culture also places great importance on hoʻoponopono, a traditional practice of reconciliation and forgiveness. This concept reflects the belief in resolving conflicts with empathy, promoting harmony in personal and community relationships. It highlights the Hawaiian approach to peace and understanding, showing how Aloha extends into every interaction.

Incorporating the Aloha Spirit into your time in Hawaii not only deepens your appreciation of the islands but also encourages you to live in a way that embodies kindness and respect. By embracing this unique cultural philosophy, you'll experience the true heart of Hawaii and its people.

# Geography and Overview of the Hawaiian Islands

The Hawaiian Islands, a breathtaking archipelago in the central Pacific Ocean, are renowned for their stunning landscapes, diverse ecosystems, and rich cultural heritage. Comprising **137 islands,** atolls, and islets, this tropical paradise is primarily made up of eight main islands: Hawaii (the Big Island), Maui, Oahu, Kauai, Molokai, Lanai, Niihau, and Kahoolawe. Each island boasts its own unique character, geography, and experiences, making Hawaii a vibrant tapestry of natural beauty and cultural diversity.

The islands were formed through volcanic activity, with the Big Island being home to Mauna Loa and Mauna Kea, two of the world's largest volcanoes. Mauna Loa, an active shield volcano, rises more than 13,000 feet above sea level, while Mauna Kea is the highest point in Hawaii and a significant site for astronomical observation. The volcanic activity has created dramatic landscapes, including lush rainforests, rugged cliffs, and expansive lava fields. The Big Island is also known for Volcanoes National Park, where visitors can witness the awe-inspiring power of nature through active lava flows and craters.

**Maui,** often referred to as the **"Valley Isle,"** features the scenic Road to Hana, a breathtaking coastal drive that takes you through lush tropical rainforests, cascading waterfalls, and picturesque beaches. Haleakalā National Park, home to the world's largest dormant volcano, offers stunning sunrise and sunset views that draw visitors from around the globe.

**Oahu,** known as the **"Gathering Place,"** is the most populous island and serves as the cultural and economic hub of Hawaii. The island features the iconic Waikiki Beach, historic Pearl Harbor, and the majestic Diamond Head crater, which offers panoramic views of Honolulu and the Pacific Ocean.

**Kauai,** dubbed the **"Garden Isle,"** is famous for its verdant landscapes, dramatic cliffs, and pristine beaches. The Napali Coast, with its towering sea cliffs and lush valleys, is a must-see for nature lovers and adventurers alike.

Molokai and Lanai offer a glimpse into traditional Hawaiian life, with a slower pace and rich agricultural history. Niihau, known as the "Forbidden Island," is privately owned and remains largely untouched by tourism, preserving its unique culture.

In summary, the Hawaiian Islands are a geographical marvel, each island contributing to the archipelago's allure with its distinct landscapes, ecosystems, and cultural heritage. From volcanic mountains to vibrant coral reefs, Hawaii's diverse geography provides an unforgettable backdrop for exploration and adventure.

## Climate and Best Time to Visit Hawaii

Hawaii boasts a tropical climate that is characterized by warm temperatures, abundant sunshine, and gentle trade winds. This idyllic weather is one of the island chain's most appealing features, making it a year-round destination for travelers seeking sun, surf, and stunning landscapes. However, understanding the seasonal variations can enhance your experience and help you choose the best time to visit.

Hawaii's climate is generally divided into two main seasons: the dry season, which runs from May to October, and the wet season, from November to April. During the dry season, average temperatures range from the mid-70s to the low 90s Fahrenheit (approximately 24 to 34 degrees Celsius), making it an ideal time for beach activities, hiking, and outdoor adventures. The warm weather and lower humidity levels also create perfect conditions for exploring the islands' natural wonders.

Conversely, the wet season brings increased rainfall, particularly on the windward (northeastern) sides of the islands, where lush rainforests thrive. Despite this, rainfall is often brief and localized, with sunny skies frequently returning shortly after. The leeward (southwestern) sides tend to be drier, making areas like Waikiki and Lahaina more appealing during this season. Average temperatures during the wet season remain comfortable, typically ranging from the low 60s to mid-80s Fahrenheit (approximately 16 to 30 degrees Celsius).

The best time to visit Hawaii largely depends on your preferences and planned activities. For those seeking ideal beach weather and outdoor exploration, the dry season is recommended. This period coincides with the peak tourist season, especially during summer and winter holidays, so expect larger crowds and higher accommodation prices.

However, if you're looking to avoid the tourist rush, consider visiting during the shoulder seasons, specifically in April to June or September to November. During these months, the weather is still pleasant, and you can enjoy fewer crowds and more competitive pricing on hotels and activities.

Additionally, if you're interested in experiencing Hawaii's unique seasonal events, such as the Merrie Monarch Festival in April or the Aloha

Festivals in September, planning your visit around these dates can provide a deeper insight into the islands' rich culture.

In summary, Hawaii's inviting climate makes it a year-round destination, but understanding the nuances of its weather can enhance your visit. Whether you're drawn to sun-soaked beaches or vibrant cultural experiences, there's a perfect time to discover the magic of these islands.

# CHAPTER 2: PLANNING YOUR TRIP

## Travel Requirements and Entry Information for Hawaii

Traveling to Hawaii is a dream for many, but it's essential to understand the travel requirements and entry information to ensure a smooth journey. As a U.S. state, Hawaii has specific regulations that visitors must follow, particularly regarding identification, health protocols, and documentation.

1. **Identification and Documentation**
For U.S. citizens traveling to Hawaii, a government-issued photo ID, such as a driver's license or passport, is required for air travel. Those flying from the U.S. mainland to Hawaii do not need a visa or any special documentation beyond their ID. However, international

travelers must have a valid passport and, depending on their country of origin, may require a visa to enter the United States. It's crucial to check with the U.S. Department of State for the latest visa requirements based on your nationality.

## 2. Health Protocols

In light of recent global events, health protocols are an important consideration. While Hawaii has lifted many COVID-19-related restrictions, travelers should stay informed about any potential requirements before their trip. As of now, there are no mandatory testing or vaccination requirements for domestic travelers. However, international travelers may need to provide proof of vaccination or a negative COVID-19 test result upon entry. It's advisable to check the Hawaii Department of Health's website or the Centers for Disease Control and Prevention (CDC) guidelines before your departure.

## 3. Travel Insurance

While not mandatory, obtaining travel insurance is highly recommended. Insurance can provide coverage for unforeseen events, such as trip cancellations, medical emergencies, or lost luggage. Having a policy that covers COVID-19-related issues can also offer added peace of mind during your travels.

## 4. Transportation and Getting Around

Upon arriving in Hawaii, visitors have various transportation options. Major airports, including Daniel K. Inouye International Airport in Honolulu and Kahului Airport on Maui, provide car rental services, shuttles, and public transportation. Renting a car is popular for those wishing to explore the islands at their own pace, while public transportation is a budget-friendly option for getting around urban areas.

## 5. Cultural Etiquette

Finally, understanding local customs and etiquette can enhance your visit. The Aloha Spirit emphasizes respect and kindness, so greeting locals with "Aloha" and being mindful of cultural practices is essential. Visitors are encouraged to embrace the spirit of ohana (family) and malama 'aina (care for the land) to fully appreciate the unique Hawaiian culture.

In conclusion, preparing for travel to Hawaii involves understanding identification requirements, health protocols, transportation options, and cultural etiquette. By planning ahead and staying informed, you can ensure a memorable and enjoyable trip to this beautiful paradise.

## Transportation: Flights, Ferries, and Local Transit in Hawaii

Traveling around Hawaii is an adventure in itself, and understanding the various transportation options available can significantly enhance your experience on these stunning islands. With their unique geography, the modes of transportation range from flights and ferries to local transit systems. Here's a breakdown of the best ways to navigate Hawaii.

## 1. **Flights Between Islands**

Given the vastness of the Hawaiian archipelago, inter-island flights are often the quickest way to travel between the islands. Several airlines, including Hawaiian Airlines, Mokulele Airlines, and Southwest Airlines, offer frequent flights connecting the main islands such as Oahu, Maui, Kauai, and the Big Island. These short flights, typically lasting around 30 to 60 minutes, provide stunning aerial views of the islands' landscapes and coastlines. Booking in advance can often yield better rates, and travelers should be aware of potential baggage fees.

## 2. **Ferries**

Ferries are another option for inter-island travel, particularly between Maui and Lanai or Molokai. The Maui-Lanai Expeditions Ferry and the Maui-Molokai Ferry operate regularly and offer a scenic way to travel while enjoying the ocean views. Ferry rides typically take about an hour and are a great alternative for those looking to avoid flying. Reservations are recommended, especially during peak travel seasons, to ensure availability.

## 3. **Local Transit**

Once you arrive on each island, local transit systems offer convenient and budget-friendly ways to explore. Oahu boasts a well-developed public bus system known as TheBus, which serves most of the island and provides access to major tourist destinations, beaches, and shopping areas. A one-way fare is economical, and a day pass allows unlimited travel for a small fee.

Maui's public transportation, known as **Maui Bus,** offers routes throughout the island, connecting key areas, including the airport and popular tourist spots. While not as extensive as Oahu's system, it is still a reliable option for visitors.

For those seeking more flexibility, renting a car is highly recommended, especially on the islands of Maui, the Big Island, and Kauai, where attractions are more spread out. Major rental car companies operate at airports and in popular towns. Having a car allows you to explore hidden gems, scenic drives, and off-the-beaten-path locations at your leisure.

4. **Biking and Walking**
Many areas, particularly in Waikiki and Lahaina, are bike-friendly, with rental shops offering bicycles and electric scooters. Walking is also a delightful way to experience local neighborhoods, shop, and dine.

In summary, transportation in Hawaii includes a variety of options to suit every traveler's needs. Whether flying between islands, taking a ferry, using local transit, or renting a car, getting around is convenient and allows you to fully immerse yourself in the natural beauty and culture of the islands.

# Budgeting and Costs: What to Expect When Traveling to Hawaii

Planning a trip to Hawaii can be exhilarating, but it's essential to understand the budgeting and costs associated with your visit to ensure a smooth and enjoyable experience. Hawaii is often regarded as one of the more expensive travel destinations in the United States, but with careful planning, you can manage your expenses while enjoying the beauty and culture of the islands.

### 1. Accommodation Costs

Accommodation can take up a significant portion of your budget. Prices vary widely based on the type of lodging, location, and season. Luxury resorts and beachfront hotels can cost anywhere from $300 to $800 per night, while mid-range hotels typically range from $150 to $300. For budget travelers, hostels and vacation rentals can be more affordable options, with prices starting around $50 per night. Booking well in advance or during the off-peak season can help you secure better rates.

## 2. Transportation Expenses

Getting around the islands is another expense to consider. Inter-island flights generally cost between $50 and $150 each way, depending on how early you book and the airline. Renting a car is advisable for exploring islands like Maui, Kauai, and the Big Island, with rental rates averaging $30 to $70 per day. Be sure to factor in gas prices, which can be higher than on the mainland.

## 3. Food and Dining

Food costs can also vary widely in Hawaii. Dining at casual restaurants can range from $15 to $30 per person for a meal, while mid-range restaurants may charge between $30 and $60 per person. For a more budget-friendly option, consider local food trucks and markets where you can find delicious meals for $10 to $15. Grocery stores offer an affordable alternative for those looking to prepare their own meals, especially if you have access to a kitchen in your accommodations.

## 4. Activities and Excursions
The cost of activities can also impact your overall budget. Many of Hawaii's natural attractions, such as beaches and hiking trails, are free or have minimal entrance fees. However, guided tours, such as snorkeling, helicopter rides, and luaus, can range from $50 to $300 per person, depending on the experience. It's wise to plan ahead and look for deals or package offers to save on excursions.

## 5. Overall Budgeting Tips
In general, a daily budget of $150 to $300 per person can be a reasonable estimate for a moderate traveler, including accommodation, meals, and activities. For a more luxurious experience, be prepared to spend $400 or more per day. To save money, consider visiting during the shoulder seasons (spring and fall) when prices are typically lower, and crowds are fewer.

In summary, understanding budgeting and costs in Hawaii is crucial for a successful trip. By planning ahead and being mindful of your spending, you can experience the islands' breathtaking beauty without breaking the bank.

## Sustainable Tourism: Responsible Travel Tips in Hawaii

As one of the most beautiful and ecologically rich destinations in the world, Hawaii faces the challenge of balancing tourism with environmental preservation. Sustainable tourism is key to protecting the islands' fragile ecosystems while ensuring future generations can enjoy their natural beauty. Here are some responsible travel tips to help you minimize your environmental impact while visiting Hawaii.

**1. Respect Local Culture and Traditions**
Hawaiian culture is deeply connected to the land and sea, with traditions emphasizing respect for

nature. Embrace the Aloha Spirit by learning about local customs and treating the environment with care. Engage with the community in respectful ways, such as attending cultural events, supporting local artisans, and understanding sacred sites like heiau (Hawaiian temples) and beaches. Always ask for permission before entering restricted or private areas.

## 2. Practice Malama 'Aina (Care for the Land)

Malama 'aina, meaning "care for the land," is a core Hawaiian value. When visiting beaches, parks, and trails, take only memories and leave only footprints. Avoid littering, and if possible, participate in beach cleanups or conservation projects that help protect Hawaii's ecosystems. Ensure you stay on designated trails when hiking to avoid damaging native plants or disturbing wildlife.

## 3. Minimize Plastic Use

Hawaii, like many island ecosystems, is particularly vulnerable to plastic pollution.

Single-use plastics can harm marine life and the environment, so consider bringing reusable water bottles, utensils, and shopping bags. Many local businesses support eco-friendly practices, so look for sustainable alternatives when shopping or dining out.

## 4. Choose Eco-Friendly Tours and Activities

Many tour operators in Hawaii prioritize environmental conservation. When booking excursions, choose companies that practice responsible tourism, such as those certified by the Hawaii Ecotourism Association. These companies ensure that their activities, such as snorkeling, whale watching, or hiking, minimize harm to the environment and educate visitors about Hawaii's unique ecosystems.

## 5. Support Local Businesses

Opt for locally-owned hotels, restaurants, and shops to support the Hawaiian economy and reduce the carbon footprint of imported goods. Buying local not only enriches your travel experience but also helps sustain the community, ensuring that tourism benefits Hawaii's residents.

6. **Reduce Energy and Water Usage**
Hawaii has limited resources, so conserving water and energy is crucial. Be mindful of your usage by taking shorter showers, turning off lights when not in use, and reusing towels and linens in your accommodations. These small actions can significantly reduce the strain on Hawaii's natural resources.

By following these responsible travel tips, you contribute to the preservation of Hawaii's environment and culture, helping ensure the islands remain a paradise for generations to come. Sustainable tourism is not only about reducing harm but also about giving back to the places that welcome us with open arms.

**Here are a few ways this response could be improved:**

Adding more in-depth details on Hawaii's most endangered species and how tourism affects them.

Including more practical examples of eco-friendly tour companies or specific programs visitors can join.

Exploring ways visitors can give back to local Hawaiian communities, beyond shopping locally.

# CHAPTER 3: THE ISLANDS OF HAWAII

## Oahu: The Gathering Place

Oahu, often referred to as **"The Gathering Place,"** is the third-largest island in the

Hawaiian archipelago and the most populous. Known for its diverse culture, stunning landscapes, and vibrant urban life, Oahu offers visitors a unique blend of natural beauty and modern conveniences. From iconic beaches to historical sites, this island is a must-visit destination for anyone traveling to Hawaii.

1. **Cultural Hub**

As the cultural and economic heart of Hawaii, Oahu is home to Honolulu, the state capital, which showcases a rich tapestry of traditions and influences. The island's diverse population includes Native Hawaiians, Asians, and Pacific Islanders, contributing to a unique cultural blend. Visitors can immerse themselves in this vibrant culture by exploring local art galleries, attending traditional hula performances, and savoring Hawaiian cuisine at family-owned restaurants.

The Bishop Museum and Iolani Palace offer insights into Hawaii's royal history and cultural heritage, while the Hawaii State Art Museum showcases contemporary Hawaiian artists. Additionally, the Aloha Festivals held in September celebrate Hawaiian culture with parades, music, and traditional hula.

## 2. Breathtaking Landscapes

Oahu is renowned for its stunning natural beauty, featuring diverse landscapes that range from lush mountains to pristine beaches. Waikiki Beach, perhaps the most famous beach in the world, attracts sunbathers, surfers, and water sports enthusiasts alike. The golden sands and clear waters make it a perfect spot for relaxation and recreation.

Beyond Waikiki, the North Shore is famous for its legendary surfing spots, particularly during the winter months when massive waves attract professional surfers from around the globe. The laid-back atmosphere and charming local shops in towns like Haleiwa add to the North Shore's appeal.

For those seeking adventure, Oahu's hiking trails offer breathtaking views of the island's topography. The hike to Diamond Head Crater rewards visitors with panoramic vistas of Honolulu and the coastline, while trails like Manoa Falls provide glimpses of the island's lush rainforests.

3. **Historical Significance**
Oahu is steeped in history, with sites like Pearl Harbor serving as powerful reminders of World War II. The USS Arizona Memorial honors the lives lost during the attack on December 7, 1941, and is a poignant tribute to those who served. Visitors can learn about the history and impact of this pivotal moment through guided tours and exhibits.

In summary, Oahu is a captivating destination that offers a perfect blend of culture, adventure, and history. As "The Gathering Place," it invites visitors to connect with the rich traditions of Hawaii while exploring its breathtaking landscapes. Whether you're looking to relax on world-famous beaches, savor local cuisine, or learn about the islands' history, Oahu promises an unforgettable experience that captures the essence of Hawaii.

## Maui: The Valley Isle

Maui, often referred to as "The Valley Isle," is the second-largest island in the Hawaiian archipelago and is renowned for its stunning landscapes, diverse ecosystems, and vibrant culture. Named for the demigod Māui, the island features a unique geography characterized by lush valleys, towering mountains, and picturesque beaches, making it a top destination for travelers seeking both adventure and relaxation.

1. **Natural Beauty**

One of Maui's most iconic features is the Haleakalā National Park, home to the world's largest dormant volcano. Rising over 10,000 feet, Haleakalā offers breathtaking sunrises and sunsets that draw visitors from around the globe. The park's diverse climate zones allow for unique ecosystems, from the arid desert at the summit to the lush rainforest at its base. Hiking trails wind through the park, showcasing rare plants and wildlife, including the endangered Hawaiian goose, or nene.

The Road to Hana is another highlight of Maui, famed for its breathtaking coastal views, cascading waterfalls, and lush rainforests. This scenic drive features 620 curves and 59 bridges, providing ample opportunities to explore charming towns, black sand beaches, and hidden waterfalls along the way. Stops at places like Waianapanapa State Park and the Seven Sacred Pools at Ohe'o Gulch are must-sees for visitors wanting to experience Maui's natural wonders.

## 2. Beaches and Water Activities

Maui boasts some of the best beaches in the world, each with its own unique charm. Kaanapali Beach, with its golden sands and crystal-clear waters, is a popular spot for sunbathing, swimming, and snorkeling. Wailea Beach, known for its luxury resorts, offers a more tranquil setting for those seeking relaxation.

Water activities abound on Maui, from snorkeling in the vibrant reefs of Molokini Crater to embarking on whale-watching tours during the winter months. The waters surrounding the island teem with marine life, making it a paradise for divers and snorkelers alike.

3. **Cultural Experience**

Maui's rich cultural heritage is deeply rooted in Hawaiian traditions. Visitors can experience this culture firsthand by attending a traditional luau, where they can enjoy hula dancing, music, and authentic Hawaiian cuisine. The island also hosts various art galleries and cultural festivals that celebrate its unique history.

In summary, Maui, "The Valley Isle," offers an enchanting blend of natural beauty, adventure, and cultural richness. Whether hiking to the summit of Haleakalā, exploring the Road to Hana, or simply relaxing on pristine beaches, Maui promises an unforgettable experience for every traveler. With its stunning landscapes and warm hospitality, it's no wonder Maui captures the hearts of all who visit.

## *Big Island (Hawaii): The Orchid Isle*

The Big Island of Hawaii, affectionately known as "The Orchid Isle," is the largest and most diverse island in the Hawaiian archipelago. Boasting a unique blend of stunning landscapes, vibrant ecosystems, and rich cultural heritage, the Big Island offers visitors an array of experiences that highlight its natural beauty and cultural significance.

## 1. Diverse Landscapes

One of the most remarkable features of the Big Island is its diverse geography, which includes everything from volcanic landscapes to lush rainforests and pristine beaches. Home to Mauna Kea, the highest peak in Hawaii, and Mauna Loa, one of the world's most active volcanoes, the island is a living testament to the power of nature. Hawai'i Volcanoes National Park is a must-visit destination, where you can witness the incredible volcanic activity that shapes the island. The park features a variety of hiking trails, allowing visitors to explore lava fields, steam vents, and lush rainforests, as well as the Kīlauea Caldera, where you can often see lava flowing into the ocean.

2. **Rich Biodiversity**

The Big Island is also home to a wide array of ecosystems, making it a haven for nature lovers. The island's varying elevations create distinct climates and habitats, supporting diverse flora and fauna. Visitors can explore Hakalau Forest National Wildlife Refuge, where they can spot endemic Hawaiian birds and unique plant species. The island's coastline offers opportunities for snorkeling and diving in vibrant coral reefs, teeming with marine life, including sea turtles and colorful fish.

3. **Cultural Heritage**

Culturally, the Big Island is rich in Hawaiian traditions and history. Pu'uhonua o Hōnaunau National Historical Park, also known as the Place of Refuge, offers insights into ancient Hawaiian society. This sacred site served as a sanctuary for those who broke kapu (ancient laws) and needed forgiveness. Visitors can explore reconstructed Hawaiian structures and learn about traditional practices through interpretive exhibits and guided tours.

The island is also famous for its thriving agricultural scene, particularly its coffee and orchid cultivation. The Kona Coffee Belt produces some of the world's finest coffee, and visitors can tour local farms to learn about the coffee-making process and enjoy tastings.

In summary, the Big Island, or "The Orchid Isle," offers a unique blend of natural wonders, cultural experiences, and outdoor adventures. Whether exploring volcanic landscapes, enjoying pristine beaches, or immersing yourself in Hawaiian traditions, the Big Island captivates every visitor with its diverse offerings. This enchanting island is truly a gem of the Hawaiian archipelago, promising unforgettable experiences and memories.

## Kauai: The Garden Isle

Kauai, often referred to as "The Garden Isle," is the oldest and fourth-largest island in the Hawaiian archipelago. Known for its lush greenery, dramatic landscapes, and rich natural beauty, Kauai is a paradise for nature lovers and adventure seekers alike. With its stunning beaches, cascading waterfalls, and vibrant rainforests, this enchanting island offers visitors a unique opportunity to immerse themselves in the pristine wilderness of Hawaii.

## 1. Lush Landscapes

Kauai is characterized by its diverse ecosystems, which range from jagged cliffs and pristine beaches to verdant valleys and fertile rainforests. One of the most iconic sights on the island is the Na Pali Coast, a breathtaking stretch of coastline featuring dramatic cliffs that rise steeply from the ocean. Visitors can explore this stunning area by hiking the Kalalau Trail, which offers awe-inspiring views of the coastline and lush landscapes. Alternatively, boat tours and helicopter rides provide a different perspective, allowing travelers to witness the coastline's grandeur from the sea or sky.

Another highlight is Waimea Canyon, often referred to as the **"Grand Canyon of the Pacific."** This remarkable geological formation features colorful ridges and deep valleys that create a stunning backdrop for hiking and photography. The canyon offers several lookout points, each providing breathtaking views of the canyon's dramatic landscapes.

## 2. Outdoor Activities

Kauai is a haven for outdoor enthusiasts, offering a myriad of activities that allow visitors to explore its natural beauty. From hiking and kayaking to snorkeling and zip-lining, the island provides endless opportunities for adventure. Hanalei Bay is a popular spot for swimming, paddleboarding, and surfing, with its picturesque beach framed by lush mountains.

The island is also home to several stunning waterfalls, including Wailua Falls and Opaekaa Falls, which are easily accessible and perfect for photography. For a more off-the-beaten-path experience, the Secret Falls hike leads adventurers through lush forests to a hidden waterfall, providing a refreshing swimming opportunity.

## 3. Cultural Heritage

Kauai's rich cultural heritage is evident in its historic sites and traditions. Visitors can explore the Kauai Museum to learn about the island's history and the significance of ancient Hawaiian practices. Additionally, local festivals celebrate Hawaiian culture through music, dance, and traditional cuisine.

In summary, Kauai, **"The Garden Isle,"** captivates visitors with its breathtaking landscapes, outdoor adventures, and rich cultural heritage. Whether hiking along the Na Pali Coast, exploring Waimea Canyon, or relaxing on pristine beaches, Kauai offers a serene escape into nature's beauty. This lush island invites you to experience the magic of Hawaii, leaving a lasting impression on all who visit.

# Lanai and Molokai: Off the Beaten Path

Lanai and Molokai, two of Hawaii's lesser-known islands, offer a unique and authentic experience for travelers seeking to escape the crowds and explore the rich culture and natural beauty of the Hawaiian archipelago. Often overshadowed by their more popular neighbors, these islands provide a serene and laid-back atmosphere, perfect for those looking to immerse themselves in the islands' tranquil charm.

## 1. **Lanai: The Pineapple Isle**

Lanai, known as the "Pineapple Isle," was once the largest pineapple plantation in the world, and remnants of its agricultural history can still be found throughout the island. Today, Lanai boasts a stunning landscape characterized by lush forests, rugged coastline, and pristine beaches.

Visitors to Lanai can explore Hulopoe Bay, a protected marine preserve ideal for snorkeling, swimming, and relaxing on the beach. The crystal-clear waters are home to a variety of marine life, including colorful fish and sea turtles. For adventure seekers, the Munro Trail offers breathtaking views of the island and the neighboring islands, making it a popular hiking destination.

One of Lanai's unique attractions is the Keahiakawelo, or the "Garden of the Gods," a striking landscape filled with colorful rock formations and lunar-like terrain. This otherworldly area is best visited during sunrise or sunset, when the colors of the rocks come alive in brilliant hues.

2. **Molokai: The Friendly Isle**

Just a short ferry ride from Lanai, Molokai is known as the "Friendly Isle" and is celebrated for its strong sense of community and deep-rooted Hawaiian culture. With its slow-paced lifestyle, Molokai offers a glimpse into traditional Hawaiian life, making it an ideal destination for those looking to connect with the local culture.

Visitors can explore Kalaupapa National Historical Park, which tells the poignant story of the leprosy settlement founded in the 19th century. The park offers guided tours that provide insight into the lives of those who lived there, emphasizing the resilience and strength of the human spirit.

For outdoor enthusiasts, Molokai boasts beautiful landscapes, including Halawa Valley, where guided hikes lead you through lush terrain to stunning waterfalls. The island's unspoiled beaches, such as Papohaku Beach, offer a serene escape for sunbathing, swimming, and picnicking.

In summary, Lanai and Molokai present a unique opportunity to experience Hawaii off the beaten path. With their stunning natural beauty, rich cultural heritage, and welcoming communities, these islands invite visitors to slow down, explore, and connect with the authentic spirit of Hawaii. Whether you're hiking through lush valleys or relaxing on secluded beaches, Lanai and Molokai promise an unforgettable journey into the heart of the Hawaiian Islands.

# CHAPTER 4: MUST-SEE NATURAL WONDERS

## Hawai'i Volcanoes National Park: A Natural Wonder

Hawai'i Volcanoes National Park, located on the Big Island, is a mesmerizing testament to the power and beauty of nature. Spanning over 323,000 acres, the park is home to two of the world's most active volcanoes: Kīlauea and Mauna Loa. This UNESCO World Heritage Site offers visitors a unique opportunity to witness volcanic activity up close while exploring diverse ecosystems, stunning landscapes, and rich cultural history.

## 1. Kīlauea: The Heart of the Park

Kīlauea, one of the most active volcanoes on the planet, serves as the park's centerpiece. The volcano has been erupting intermittently for over three decades, creating a dynamic landscape that changes constantly. Visitors can access the Kīlauea Visitor Center to learn about the volcano's geology, history, and recent eruptions. From there, a short drive or hike leads to Crater Rim Drive, where you can view the Kīlauea Caldera and the steaming Halemaʻumaʻu Crater, which has become a significant cultural site for Native Hawaiians.

One of the park's highlights is the Chain of Craters Road, a scenic route that descends from the summit of Kīlauea to the coastline. Along the way, visitors can explore various hiking trails and view unique geological features, including old lava flows and colorful craters.

## 2. Mauna Loa: The Mighty Giant

Mauna Loa, the largest volcano on Earth by volume, is also within the park. While it is less frequently active than Kīlauea, its sheer size and geological significance make it an awe-inspiring sight. The Mauna Loa Observatory offers educational insights into climate and atmospheric studies, showcasing the importance of this region in global research.

## 3. Diverse Ecosystems

Beyond the volcanic landscapes, the park boasts an impressive array of ecosystems, ranging from lush rainforests to barren lava fields. Hiking through the Thurston Lava Tube, a natural tunnel formed by flowing lava, provides a fascinating glimpse into the park's volcanic activity. Trails like the Kīlauea Iki Trail lead you through native forests filled with unique flora and fauna, including endangered species.

### 4. Cultural Significance

Hawai'i Volcanoes National Park is also rich in cultural heritage. The park holds significant spiritual importance for Native Hawaiians, who believe that the goddess Pele resides in Kīlauea. Numerous petroglyphs and archaeological sites throughout the park tell stories of the island's history and its connection to the land.

In summary, Hawai'i Volcanoes National Park is a breathtaking destination that showcases the raw power of nature and the beauty of the Hawaiian landscape. Whether you're hiking through lush rainforests, observing volcanic activity, or learning about the island's cultural significance, the park offers an unforgettable experience that highlights the unique geology and heritage of the Big Island.

## Na Pali Coast: Kauai's Breathtaking Jewel

The Na Pali Coast, a stunning 17-mile stretch of rugged cliffs and lush valleys on the north shore of Kauai, is one of Hawaii's most iconic natural wonders. Known for its dramatic scenery, vibrant green landscapes, and crystal-clear waters, this breathtaking coastline is a must-visit destination for travelers seeking adventure and beauty in one of the most picturesque settings in the world.

1. **Spectacular Scenery**

The Na Pali Coast is characterized by its steep, emerald-green cliffs that rise abruptly from the Pacific Ocean, creating a striking contrast against the deep blue waters. The coastline features numerous valleys, waterfalls, and secluded beaches, making it a visual feast for visitors. Notable landmarks include the famous Kalalau Valley, which is home to lush vegetation and stunning vistas, and Hanakapiai Falls, a majestic waterfall that cascades into a pristine pool surrounded by dense forest.

2. **Adventure Awaits**

For those looking to explore this natural paradise, there are several ways to experience the Na Pali Coast. The Kalalau Trail, a challenging 11-mile hike, offers hikers the opportunity to traverse the coastline and witness breathtaking views of the cliffs and valleys. Along the way, hikers will encounter lush rainforests, rocky landscapes, and stunning beaches, making it a rewarding journey for outdoor enthusiasts.

Alternatively, guided boat tours allow visitors to view the coastline from the water, providing a different perspective of the dramatic cliffs and hidden sea caves. Many tour operators offer snorkeling excursions, enabling visitors to explore the vibrant marine life in the surrounding waters. For a truly unforgettable experience, helicopter tours offer breathtaking aerial views of the Na Pali Coast, showcasing its majestic beauty from above.

### 3. Wildlife and Conservation

The Na Pali Coast is also home to diverse wildlife, including seabirds, dolphins, and, during certain seasons, migrating humpback whales. Efforts to conserve this pristine environment are vital, as it is considered one of the last remaining natural habitats in Hawaii. Visitors are encouraged to respect the land, practice Leave No Trace principles, and participate in local conservation initiatives.

In summary, the Na Pali Coast is a breathtaking jewel of Kauai, offering visitors unparalleled natural beauty and outdoor adventure. Whether hiking the Kalalau Trail, taking a boat tour, or admiring the stunning vistas from above, the Na Pali Coast promises an unforgettable experience that captures the essence of Hawaii's enchanting landscapes. This extraordinary coastline is a testament to the power of nature and a must-see for anyone visiting the Garden Isle.

# Haleakalā National Park: Maui's Majestic Volcano

Haleakalā National Park, located on the Hawaiian island of Maui, is a stunning testament to the power of nature and the beauty of volcanic landscapes. Spanning over 30,000 acres, this diverse park is home to the majestic Haleakalā volcano, which rises 10,023 feet above sea level, making it one of the highest points in Hawaii. Renowned for its breathtaking sunrises, unique ecosystems, and rich cultural history, Haleakalā National Park offers a wealth of experiences for nature lovers and adventurers alike.

## 1. A Dramatic Landscape

At the heart of the park lies the massive summit caldera, a volcanic crater measuring over 2.5 miles wide and surrounded by rugged terrain. The landscape is characterized by its otherworldly beauty, with a patchwork of colorful cinder cones, lava fields, and native vegetation. The park's elevation creates diverse microclimates, ranging from arid desert-like conditions at the summit to lush rainforests at lower elevations. This variety supports a rich array of flora and fauna, including many endemic species that are found nowhere else on Earth.

## 2. Breathtaking Sunrises and Sunsets

One of the park's most popular attractions is the breathtaking sunrise and sunset views from the summit of Haleakalā. Visitors often wake before dawn to witness the spectacular transformation of the landscape as the sun rises above the clouds, casting vibrant colors across the sky. The experience is awe-inspiring, drawing crowds eager to witness this natural spectacle. For those who prefer the quiet of the evening, sunsets at Haleakalā are equally enchanting, offering a tranquil atmosphere as the sun dips below the horizon.

## 3. Outdoor Activities

Haleakalā National Park is a haven for outdoor enthusiasts, offering numerous hiking trails that showcase the park's stunning landscapes and unique ecosystems. The Sliding Sands Trail provides an opportunity to hike into the crater, while trails like the Pipiwai Trail lead through lush bamboo forests to the breathtaking Waimoku Falls. For stargazing enthusiasts, the park is designated as a Dark Sky Reserve, making it an ideal location to marvel at the night sky, far away from city lights.

4. **Cultural Significance**

Haleakalā holds deep cultural significance for Native Hawaiians, who consider the volcano sacred. The park is rich in Hawaiian history and mythology, with stories of the demigod Maui and the creation of the Hawaiian Islands deeply embedded in the landscape. Visitors are encouraged to respect the land and its cultural heritage while exploring this magnificent natural wonder.

In summary, Haleakalā National Park is a breathtaking destination that showcases the diverse beauty of Maui's volcanic landscapes.

From stunning sunrises and sunsets to unique ecosystems and rich cultural heritage, the park offers an unforgettable experience for every visitor. Whether you're hiking through its diverse trails or simply soaking in the stunning views, Haleakalā National Park is a testament to the natural wonders of Hawaii.

## Waimea Canyon: The Grand Canyon of the Pacific

Waimea Canyon, often referred to as the "Grand Canyon of the Pacific," is one of Kauai's most breathtaking natural wonders. Stretching over 14 miles long, up to 1 mile wide, and more than 3,600 feet deep, this stunning geological marvel showcases the island's dramatic landscape and rich geological history. Carved by centuries of erosion and the forces of nature, Waimea Canyon offers visitors a spectacular view of vibrant colors, lush vegetation, and striking rock formations.

1. **Dramatic Landscapes**

The canyon's walls are adorned with a mosaic of reds, oranges, and greens, creating a stunning visual contrast against the blue skies. The colorful layers of volcanic rock tell a story that dates back millions of years, revealing the island's geological evolution. Numerous lookout points provide visitors with stunning vistas of the canyon, each offering a unique perspective of its grandeur. Popular spots like the Waimea Canyon Lookout and the Puu Hinai Lookout allow for breathtaking panoramic views that are perfect for photography and simply soaking in the beauty of the landscape.

2. **Hiking and Outdoor Adventures**

For those looking to explore more intimately, Waimea Canyon offers a variety of hiking trails that cater to different skill levels. The Canyon Trail leads to Waipo'o Falls, where hikers can enjoy a refreshing view of the cascading waterfall surrounded by lush greenery. More experienced hikers can tackle the Awa'awapuhi

Trail, which descends into a breathtaking valley and provides stunning views of the Na Pali Coast from above. These trails offer not only a chance to experience the canyon's beauty up close but also the opportunity to encounter native flora and fauna.

### 3. **Cultural Significance**

Waimea Canyon is not just a natural wonder; it also holds cultural significance for the Native Hawaiian people. The area is steeped in history, with legends that speak of its creation and the ancestors who once inhabited the region. Visitors can gain insight into the cultural heritage of Kauai by exploring the nearby Koke'e State Park, which features additional trails and historical sites that connect to the island's rich past.

In summary, Waimea Canyon is a must-visit destination for anyone traveling to Kauai. With its breathtaking vistas, diverse hiking opportunities, and rich cultural significance, the canyon offers an unforgettable experience that showcases the island's natural beauty. Whether you're standing at a lookout, hiking a scenic trail, or simply enjoying the vibrant landscapes, Waimea Canyon embodies the spirit of Hawaii and the incredible power of nature.

## Beaches and Bays: Best Spots for Sun and Sand in Hawaii

Hawaii is renowned for its stunning beaches and picturesque bays, attracting sun-seekers and adventure enthusiasts from around the globe. With its crystal-clear waters, soft golden sands, and breathtaking coastal landscapes, the islands offer some of the best beach experiences in the world. From the lively shores of Oahu to the tranquil hidden gems of Kauai, here are some of the best spots for sun and sand across the Hawaiian Islands.

## 1. **Oahu: Waikiki Beach**

Waikiki Beach is perhaps the most famous beach in Hawaii, known for its vibrant atmosphere and stunning views of Diamond Head. With its gentle waves, it's an ideal spot for swimming, surfing, and sunbathing. The beach is lined with luxurious resorts, restaurants, and shops, making it a lively hub for both locals and tourists. As the sun sets, Waikiki transforms into a magical scene, with beachgoers gathering to enjoy the golden hues of the sky and live music from nearby venues.

## 2. **Maui: Kaanapali Beach**

On Maui, Kaanapali Beach is a must-visit destination known for its pristine sands and crystal-clear waters. This beach offers excellent opportunities for snorkeling, with vibrant coral reefs teeming with marine life just offshore. The beachfront promenade is perfect for a leisurely stroll, and the nearby Black Rock is famous for cliff diving. Kaanapali is also home to several upscale resorts and restaurants, making it a great spot for both relaxation and entertainment.

### 3. Kauai: Hanalei Bay

Hanalei Bay, located on the north shore of Kauai, is often considered one of the most beautiful beaches in Hawaii. Surrounded by lush mountains and the picturesque town of Hanalei, this crescent-shaped bay offers calm waters perfect for swimming and paddleboarding. The golden sand and stunning scenery make it an ideal spot for sunbathing and picnicking. In the winter months, the bay attracts surfers eager to ride the larger waves, while the summer months offer a calmer experience for families.

### 4. Big Island: Punalu'u Black Sand Beach

For a unique beach experience, Punalu'u Black Sand Beach on the Big Island is a must-see. Formed by volcanic activity, the black sand is a striking contrast to the turquoise waters. This beach is a great spot for sunbathing and observing sea turtles that often come ashore to bask in the sun. The surrounding palm trees and scenic coastline provide a stunning backdrop for photos.

In conclusion, Hawaii's beaches and bays offer a diverse range of experiences for every type of traveler. Whether you're looking for the vibrant energy of Waikiki, the tranquil beauty of Hanalei Bay, or the unique allure of Punalu'u Black Sand Beach, the islands promise unforgettable moments under the sun. With its breathtaking natural beauty and warm, inviting waters, Hawaii is truly a beach lover's paradise.

# CHAPTER 5: CULTURAL AND HISTORICAL SITES

## *Pearl Harbor and WWII History: A Crucial Chapter in Oahu*

Pearl Harbor, located on the island of Oahu, is a site of immense historical significance, known primarily for the surprise military attack by the Japanese Imperial Navy on December 7, 1941. This pivotal event thrust the United States into World War II and marked a turning point in both American and global history. Today, Pearl Harbor serves as a memorial and educational site, allowing visitors to reflect on the sacrifices made during this tumultuous time.

### 1. Historical Significance
The attack on Pearl Harbor was a meticulously planned military operation aimed at crippling the U.S. Pacific Fleet. On that fateful day, over 350

Japanese aircraft launched an assault on the naval base, resulting in the destruction of numerous battleships, aircraft, and significant loss of life. The surprise attack killed 2,403 Americans and wounded over 1,000, profoundly impacting the nation and leading to widespread calls for retaliation.

2. **Visiting Pearl Harbor**

Today, Pearl Harbor is home to several important memorials and museums that honor the lives lost and educate visitors about the events of World War II. The USS Arizona Memorial is perhaps the most iconic site. Built over the sunken remains of the battleship USS Arizona, which was destroyed during the attack, this memorial serves as a solemn tribute to the 1,177 sailors and Marines who lost their lives on that day. Visitors can take a short boat ride to the memorial and view the wreckage of the ship below the water's surface, an emotional reminder of the tragedy.

The Pearl Harbor Visitor Center offers extensive exhibits detailing the events leading up to the attack and the broader context of World War II. Multimedia displays, photographs, and personal stories provide insights into the lives of those who experienced the war. The center also features a documentary film that chronicles the events of December 7, 1941, enhancing the visitor experience.

### 3. Other Historic Sites

In addition to the USS Arizona Memorial, Pearl Harbor is home to other significant sites, including the USS Missouri, the battleship where Japan formally surrendered in 1945, and the Pacific Aviation Museum, which showcases aircraft from the era and highlights the importance of air power during the war.

In conclusion, Pearl Harbor is a poignant reminder of the sacrifices made during World War II and a crucial part of American history. Visiting this hallowed ground allows individuals to honor those who served, learn about the complexities of war, and reflect on the impact of that fateful day. For anyone traveling to Oahu, Pearl Harbor is not just a historical site; it is a place of remembrance and education that continues to resonate with visitors from around the world.

# 'Iolani Palace and Hawaiian Royal History: A Glimpse into the Monarchy

Located in the heart of Honolulu on the island of Oahu, 'Iolani Palace stands as a symbol of Hawaii's royal heritage and rich history. As the only royal palace in the United States, it offers a unique glimpse into the lives of Hawaii's last reigning monarchs and the vibrant culture that shaped the islands.

1. **Historical Significance**
Constructed between 1879 and 1882, 'Iolani Palace served as the official residence of King

Kalākaua and later his sister, Queen Liliʻuokalani. The palace is an architectural masterpiece, blending Renaissance and American styles, and features intricate details that reflect the grandeur of the Hawaiian monarchy. It was the center of political and social life in Hawaii during the late 19th century, hosting dignitaries and world leaders.

The palace's significance extends beyond its stunning architecture. It was here that King Kalākaua worked to revive Hawaiian traditions and culture, promoting the arts and encouraging the establishment of a vibrant Hawaiian identity. Queen Liliʻuokalani, the last monarch of Hawaii, furthered this vision, but her reign was cut short by a coup d'état in 1893, leading to the overthrow of the Hawaiian monarchy and the eventual annexation of Hawaii by the United States.

2. **Exploring the Palace**
Today, ʻIolani Palace is a National Historic Landmark and serves as a museum open to the

public. Guided tours take visitors through the elegantly restored rooms, including the Throne Room, where the king and queen held court, and the State Dining Room, which showcases the opulence of royal gatherings. The palace's interior is adorned with rich woodwork, original furnishings, and historical artifacts, providing insight into the lifestyle and legacy of the Hawaiian monarchy.

### 3. Cultural Importance

Visiting 'Iolani Palace offers a deeper understanding of Hawaiian history and the importance of preserving its heritage. The site stands as a testament to the resilience of the Hawaiian people and their enduring spirit. The stories of the monarchy, particularly the struggles faced by Queen Lili'uokalani, resonate with many today, symbolizing the ongoing fight for cultural recognition and sovereignty.

In conclusion, 'Iolani Palace is more than just an architectural gem; it is a poignant reminder of Hawaii's royal past and the cultural richness that defines the islands. Exploring the palace provides visitors with a unique opportunity to connect with the history of Hawaii and reflect on the legacy of its last reigning monarchs. A visit to ʻIolani Palace is essential for anyone looking to understand the true essence of Hawaii's heritage and the enduring impact of its royal history.

## Puʻuhonua o Hōnaunau National Historical Park: A Sacred Sanctuary

Puʻuhonua o Hōnaunau National Historical Park, located on the Big Island of Hawaii, is a remarkable site that preserves the rich cultural heritage and history of the Hawaiian people. Once a sanctuary for those who broke the kapu (ancient laws), this sacred place served as a refuge where individuals could seek forgiveness and avoid punishment. Today, the park stands as a testament to Hawaii's unique cultural legacy, offering visitors a glimpse into the island's ancient practices and spiritual beliefs.

## 1. Historical Significance

Established as a national historical park in 1961, Puʻuhonua o Hōnaunau encompasses approximately 420 acres of lush landscape, including coastal areas, sacred sites, and the remnants of ancient Hawaiian structures. The park's name translates to "place of refuge," reflecting its historical role as a sanctuary for individuals who transgressed kapu. These laws governed various aspects of Hawaiian life, and breaking them often resulted in severe punishment. Seeking refuge in Puʻuhonua allowed individuals to be absolved and eventually reintegrated into society after a period of purification.

## 2. Exploring the Park

Visitors to Puʻuhonua o Hōnaunau can explore a variety of significant features, including the reconstructed heiau (temples) and kiʻi (wooden images), which played a central role in ancient

Hawaiian spirituality. The Great Wall, a massive structure made of lava rock, serves as a striking reminder of the ingenuity and craftsmanship of the ancient Hawaiians. This wall demarcates the sacred space of the puʻuhonua from the surrounding area.

The park also offers several walking trails that wind through the lush landscape, providing opportunities to observe native flora and fauna. One popular trail leads to the coastline, where visitors can enjoy stunning ocean views and witness sea turtles basking on the shores.

### 3. Cultural Experiences

To enhance the visitor experience, the park often hosts cultural demonstrations and programs, allowing guests to learn traditional Hawaiian practices, such as hula, lei-making, and the art of fishnet weaving. These activities promote a deeper understanding of Hawaiian culture and history, connecting visitors to the island's heritage.

In summary, Puʻuhonua o Hōnaunau National Historical Park is a vital link to Hawaii's past, offering insights into the traditions, beliefs, and resilience of its people. Whether exploring the sacred sites, enjoying the natural beauty, or participating in cultural demonstrations, visitors to this remarkable park can gain a profound appreciation for Hawaii's rich history and the significance of this sacred sanctuary. A visit to Puʻuhonua o Hōnaunau is not just an exploration of the land but a journey into the heart of Hawaiian culture and spirituality.

## *Polynesian Cultural Center: A Celebration of Pacific Heritage*

The Polynesian Cultural Center **(PCC),** located on the north shore of Oahu, is a vibrant homage to the rich cultural heritage of the Pacific Islands. Established in 1963, this immersive cultural experience offers visitors an opportunity to explore the diverse traditions, arts, and lifestyles of Polynesia through engaging exhibits, performances, and authentic experiences. It serves as both an educational facility and a tourist attraction, drawing visitors from around the world to learn about the unique cultures of Hawaii, Samoa, Tahiti, Fiji, Tonga, and Aotearoa (New Zealand).

## 1. Cultural Exhibits and Demonstrations

At the heart of the Polynesian Cultural Center are its eight themed villages, each representing a different Polynesian culture. Visitors can explore these villages and engage with local artisans and cultural practitioners. Each village features interactive exhibits that showcase traditional crafts, dance, and music, allowing guests to participate in activities such as hula dancing, lei making, and wood carving.

One of the highlights of the PCC is the Hawaiian Village, where visitors can learn about ancient Hawaiian practices, including fishing and agriculture. The Samoan Village offers an exciting demonstration of fire-making techniques and traditional tattooing, while the Tahiti Village showcases the graceful movements of Tahitian dance. Each experience provides insight into the values, customs, and daily lives of the Polynesian people.

## 2. Evening Luau and Night Show

As the sun sets, the Polynesian Cultural Center transforms into a dazzling spectacle with its famous evening luau and show, "Hā: Breath of Life." Guests are treated to a lavish buffet featuring traditional Hawaiian cuisine, including kalua pig, poi, and tropical fruits. The luau is accompanied by captivating performances that highlight the storytelling traditions of Polynesia through music, dance, and fire knife performances.

The night show culminates in a breathtaking display of Polynesian culture, with each island's unique heritage showcased through vibrant performances. The storytelling journey brings to life the spirit of Polynesia, celebrating the interconnectedness of its people and cultures.

In summary, the Polynesian Cultural Center is a must-visit destination for anyone traveling to Oahu. It offers a unique opportunity to immerse oneself in the rich traditions of the Pacific Islands while promoting cultural understanding and appreciation. Whether exploring the themed villages, participating in hands-on activities, or enjoying the captivating evening show, visitors will leave with a deeper understanding of Polynesian culture and the shared heritage that connects these beautiful islands. The PCC is not just a tourist attraction; it is a celebration of the spirit and history of the Polynesian people.

## Native Hawaiian Traditions and Cultural Experiences: A Living Legacy

Native Hawaiian culture is rich, vibrant, and deeply connected to the land, sea, and spirit of the islands. Rooted in centuries of history and tradition, the practices of Native Hawaiians reflect a profound respect for their environment and a strong sense of community. Visitors to Hawaii have the unique opportunity to engage with these traditions and experiences, gaining insight into a culture that continues to thrive.

1. **Cultural Values and Beliefs**

At the heart of Native Hawaiian culture is the concept of aloha, which encompasses love, compassion, and respect for others. Aloha is not just a greeting; it is a guiding principle that influences how Hawaiians interact with each other and their environment. Another significant aspect is kapu, the ancient system of laws and sacred practices that governed daily life, ensuring harmony within the community and with nature.

2. **Traditional Arts and Crafts**

Visitors can explore Native Hawaiian traditions through various arts and crafts, including weaving, carving, and tattooing. The art of hula, often referred to as the language of the Hawaiian people, is a powerful form of storytelling that expresses emotions, history, and spirituality. Hula performances incorporate chants (oli) and movements that connect dancers to their ancestors and the natural world.

Workshops and cultural centers across the islands offer hands-on experiences where visitors can learn these traditional crafts. For instance, lei making—the art of crafting floral garlands—is a cherished practice that symbolizes love and affection. Participants can gather native flowers and leaves, learning about their significance and uses in Hawaiian culture.

### 3. Culinary Traditions

Native Hawaiian cuisine is another essential aspect of cultural experiences, showcasing the islands' unique flavors and ingredients. Traditional dishes like poi, made from taro root, and kalua pig, cooked in an underground oven (imu), reflect the agricultural practices and communal spirit of Hawaiian culture. Visitors can enjoy these dishes at local luaus, which often include traditional music and dance, providing a holistic cultural experience.

## 4. Ceremonial Practices and Festivals

Throughout the year, various festivals and ceremonies celebrate Native Hawaiian traditions, such as Merrie Monarch Festival, dedicated to hula and Hawaiian arts. Events like hoʻolauleʻa (cultural festivals) offer opportunities to witness traditional performances, learn about cultural practices, and engage with the local community.

In conclusion, Native Hawaiian traditions and cultural experiences provide a window into the island's rich heritage and enduring spirit. By participating in these practices, visitors gain a deeper appreciation for the culture, values, and beliefs that shape the lives of Native Hawaiians today. Engaging with this living legacy allows for meaningful connections with the land, the people, and the traditions that continue to thrive in Hawaii.

# CHAPTER 6: OUTDOOR ADVENTURES AND ACTIVITIES

## *Hiking Trails in Hawaii: From Easy to Extreme*

Hawaii, with its breathtaking landscapes and diverse ecosystems, is a hiker's paradise. The islands boast an array of hiking trails that cater to all skill levels, from leisurely walks along the coast to challenging treks through rugged terrain. Whether you're a beginner looking for a gentle stroll or an experienced hiker seeking an adrenaline-pumping adventure, Hawaii has something to offer everyone.

**1. Easy Trails: Perfect for Families and Beginners**

For those new to hiking or families with young children, several easy trails provide stunning views without the strenuous effort. The Makena Beach to Little Beach trail on Maui is a scenic coastal path that spans about 1.5 miles, offering beautiful ocean vistas and the chance to spot sea turtles along the way. Another popular choice is the Waikiki Diamond Head Crater Trail on Oahu, which is a short, well-maintained hike of approximately 1.6 miles round-trip. The trail leads to the summit of Diamond Head, rewarding hikers with panoramic views of Honolulu and the Pacific Ocean.

2. **Moderate Trails: A Bit More Challenge**
For those looking to increase the intensity of their hiking experience, several moderate trails provide a satisfying workout while still being accessible. The Koko Crater Trail, also on Oahu, is a challenging but rewarding hike that involves climbing over 1,000 steps made of railroad ties to reach the summit. The stunning views of the island and the ocean from the top make it worth the effort. On the Big Island, the Pololu Valley

Lookout Trail offers a beautiful hike down to the valley floor, where hikers can enjoy dramatic coastal views and lush greenery.

3. **Extreme Trails: For the Adventurous**
For seasoned hikers seeking extreme challenges, Hawaii offers some breathtaking and demanding trails. The Kalalau Trail on Kauai is one of the most famous, winding along the stunning Na Pali Coast. This 11-mile trail features steep ascents and descents, crossing lush valleys and rocky outcrops. The trek culminates at Kalalau Beach, a remote and stunning location only accessible by foot or boat. The Mauna Kea Summit Trail on the Big Island is another extreme option, where hikers ascend to over 13,000 feet, experiencing drastic changes in climate and terrain. The summit rewards adventurers with otherworldly landscapes and mesmerizing sunset views.

In conclusion, Hawaii's diverse hiking trails cater to all levels of hikers, making it a premier destination for outdoor enthusiasts. Whether you opt for a leisurely stroll or a challenging trek, each hike offers unique rewards, including breathtaking scenery, encounters with native wildlife, and the opportunity to connect with the islands' natural beauty. The trails of Hawaii invite everyone to explore, discover, and embrace the spirit of adventure.

## Water Sports in Hawaii: Surfing, Snorkeling, and Diving

Hawaii, often referred to as the "Aloha State," is not only famous for its stunning landscapes and rich culture but also for its incredible water sports. The islands' warm tropical waters, vibrant marine life, and consistent waves make it a paradise for surfing, snorkeling, and diving enthusiasts. Whether you're a seasoned pro or a beginner, Hawaii offers a plethora of options to explore its aquatic wonders.

### 1. Surfing: The Soul of Hawaii

Surfing is more than just a sport in Hawaii; it's a way of life and an integral part of the islands' culture. Hawaii is considered the birthplace of modern surfing, with legendary surf spots like Waikiki Beach, Banzai Pipeline, and Waimea Bay attracting surfers from around the world. Beginners can take lessons from local instructors at calmer beaches like Waikiki, where the gentle waves provide an excellent environment to learn the basics. For seasoned surfers, winter months bring swells that challenge even the most skilled surfers, making spots like the North Shore of Oahu a must-visit destination.

## 2. Snorkeling: Exploring Underwater Wonders

Snorkeling in Hawaii offers a chance to discover the vibrant underwater ecosystems teeming with colorful fish, coral reefs, and other marine life. Popular snorkeling locations include Hanauma Bay on Oahu, a protected marine life conservation area, and Molokini Crater off the coast of Maui, known for its crystal-clear waters and diverse marine life. Guided tours are widely available, often including gear rentals and instruction for beginners. Snorkelers can expect to see everything from schools of tropical fish to sea turtles and even manta rays, making it an unforgettable experience.

3. **Diving: Adventures Below the Surface**
For those seeking a more immersive underwater experience, scuba diving in Hawaii is truly exceptional. With its diverse marine habitats, the islands offer numerous diving sites, including Kona on the Big Island, where divers can encounter manta rays, dolphins, and vibrant coral reefs. The USS YO-257, a sunken ship off the coast of Oahu, provides a fascinating dive site filled with marine life and historical significance. Numerous dive shops and schools cater to divers of all skill levels, offering guided tours and certification courses.

In conclusion, Hawaii is a premier destination for water sports enthusiasts, offering exceptional opportunities for surfing, snorkeling, and diving. Whether you're riding the waves at a legendary surf spot, exploring the colorful underwater world, or embarking on a scuba diving adventure, the islands provide endless opportunities to connect with the ocean. With its warm waters, stunning marine life, and diverse environments, Hawaii invites you to dive in and embrace the thrill of water sports.

## Whale Watching and Wildlife Tours in Hawaii: A Natural Spectacle

Hawaii is renowned not only for its stunning landscapes and rich culture but also for its diverse marine life and vibrant ecosystems. Among the most awe-inspiring experiences in the Aloha State are whale watching and wildlife tours, offering visitors the chance to observe magnificent creatures in their natural habitats. The waters surrounding the islands serve as a seasonal home for humpback whales, making Hawaii one of the best places in the world to witness these gentle giants up close.

## 1. Whale Watching: A Seasonal Spectacle

From December to April, the waters around Hawaii come alive with the migration of humpback whales, which travel thousands of miles from their feeding grounds in Alaska to breed and calve in the warm, sheltered waters of the islands. Whale watching tours operate from various locations, including Maui, Oahu, and the Big Island, providing opportunities for visitors to see these majestic animals in action.

During these tours, experienced guides educate participants about the behavior and biology of humpback whales, sharing fascinating insights into their songs, breaching, and tail-slapping displays. Many tours also incorporate eco-friendly practices, ensuring minimal disruption to the whales' natural behavior. From the comfort of a boat, guests can witness the awe-inspiring sight of these massive creatures breaching the surface, often accompanied by their playful calves, creating unforgettable memories.

## 2. Wildlife Tours: Discovering Hawaii's Unique Ecosystem

In addition to whale watching, Hawaii offers a variety of wildlife tours that showcase the islands' unique fauna and flora. The diverse ecosystems found in Hawaii are home to numerous endemic species, making it a paradise for nature lovers. Guided tours can take visitors through lush rainforests, volcanic landscapes, and coastal areas, where they can spot native birds such as the 'i'iwi and the nene (Hawaiian goose).

Birdwatching tours provide an opportunity to see these beautiful species up close, while nature hikes allow for an exploration of the islands' rich biodiversity. For those interested in marine life, snorkeling and diving tours reveal colorful coral reefs, sea turtles, and schools of tropical fish.

## 3. Conservation Efforts and Education

Many tour operators in Hawaii are committed to conservation and education, emphasizing the importance of protecting marine and wildlife habitats. Through guided experiences, visitors learn about the threats facing these species and the efforts being made to preserve their ecosystems.

In summary, whale watching and wildlife tours in Hawaii offer visitors an incredible opportunity to connect with nature and witness the beauty of the islands' diverse ecosystems. Whether observing the majestic humpback whales during their migration or exploring the unique wildlife that calls Hawaii home, these experiences create lasting memories and foster a deeper appreciation for the natural world. Engaging in these activities not only enriches your visit to Hawaii but also supports the conservation of its remarkable wildlife.

# Ziplining, ATV Tours, and Helicopter Rides

Hawaii is a tropical paradise renowned for its breathtaking landscapes and vibrant ecosystems, making it an ideal destination for adventure seekers. For those looking to experience the islands from thrilling new perspectives, ziplining, ATV tours, and helicopter rides offer unforgettable adventures that showcase the stunning beauty of Hawaii's diverse terrains.

### 1. Ziplining: Soaring Above Paradise

Ziplining in Hawaii provides a unique way to experience the islands' lush landscapes from an aerial perspective. This exhilarating activity allows participants to glide through treetops and over valleys, often with stunning views of waterfalls, mountains, and the Pacific Ocean. Locations like Kauai's Zipline Tours and Maui's Skyline Eco-Adventures offer well-designed courses that cater to both beginners and experienced adventurers. Many zipline experiences also incorporate educational elements, teaching participants about the local flora and fauna as they soar above the canopy.

## 2. **ATV Tours: Off-Road Adventures**

For those who prefer a more hands-on adventure, ATV tours provide an exciting way to explore Hawaii's rugged terrains. These guided excursions take participants through diverse landscapes, including red dirt trails, coastal views, and scenic valleys. On the Big Island, Kohala ATV Tours offer thrilling rides through historical sites and breathtaking scenery, while Maui's Kahoma Ranch provides an adrenaline-pumping journey through lush landscapes.

ATV tours often combine fun with education, as guides share insights into the islands' history, geology, and ecology. Participants can expect to get muddy while navigating through trails, all while enjoying the stunning views that make Hawaii a breathtaking backdrop for adventure.

### 3. Helicopter Rides: A Bird's-Eye View

Helicopter rides in Hawaii offer a once-in-a-lifetime opportunity to witness the islands' beauty from above. These scenic flights provide breathtaking views of the dramatic landscapes, including towering cliffs, cascading waterfalls, and active volcanoes. Tour companies like Blue Hawaiian Helicopters and Maverick Helicopters offer a variety of packages, ranging from short tours to extended excursions that include remote and hard-to-reach areas.

During the flight, knowledgeable pilots provide insights into the history and geology of the islands, making the experience not only visually stunning but also educational. The aerial perspective allows visitors to appreciate the true scale and beauty of Hawaii's natural wonders.

In conclusion, ziplining, ATV tours, and helicopter rides provide thrilling ways to explore Hawaii's diverse landscapes and create unforgettable memories. Whether soaring above lush treetops, racing through rugged trails, or gliding over stunning coastlines, each adventure offers a unique perspective on the islands' natural beauty. Embracing these exciting activities allows visitors to connect with Hawaii's extraordinary environment while experiencing the thrill of adventure in paradise.

## *Golfing in Paradise: Top Golf Courses in Hawaii*

Hawaii, known for its stunning landscapes, vibrant culture, and rich history, is also a premier destination for golf enthusiasts. The islands boast some of the most breathtaking golf courses in the world, set against backdrops of lush mountains, pristine beaches, and the sparkling Pacific Ocean. Whether you're a seasoned golfer or a beginner, Hawaii offers an array of courses that cater to all skill levels, providing an unforgettable golfing experience in paradise.

### 1. Kapalua Resort (Maui)

Home to the PGA Tour's Sentry Tournament of Champions, the Kapalua Resort features two exceptional courses: the Plantation Course and the Bay Course. The Plantation Course, known for its dramatic elevation changes and stunning ocean views, is a must-play for any golfer. With its challenging holes and beautifully manicured fairways, it offers a true test of skill. The Bay Course, on the other hand, provides a more relaxed atmosphere, with its scenic views of the ocean and the surrounding mountains, making it perfect for golfers of all levels.

**2. Wailea Golf Club (Maui)**
The Wailea Golf Club features three championship courses: Blue, Gold, and Emerald. Each course offers a unique layout and stunning vistas. The Blue Course, with its picturesque ocean views, is often favored for its beautiful design and playability. The Gold Course, known for its challenging holes and lush landscapes, has hosted several prestigious tournaments, while the Emerald Course features more forgiving

fairways, making it ideal for beginners and casual players.

## 3. **Ko Olina Golf Club (Oahu)**
Located on Oahu's leeward coast, the Ko Olina Golf Club is a beautiful course designed by the legendary Ted Robinson. This 18-hole championship course is known for its lush landscaping, stunning lagoons, and challenging holes. The layout seamlessly integrates natural water features, providing a scenic and challenging round of golf. The club also offers excellent amenities, including a driving range and a pro shop, making it a perfect destination for golf lovers.

## 4. **Mauna Kea Golf Course (Big Island)**
Nestled on the Big Island, the Mauna Kea Golf Course is famous for its breathtaking views of the ocean and its challenging layout designed by Robert Trent Jones Sr. This course features elevated greens, strategically placed bunkers, and spectacular ocean views on nearly every hole. Playing at Mauna Kea is an unforgettable

experience, especially as you watch the sun set over the Pacific after your round.

In conclusion, golfing in Hawaii is an extraordinary experience that combines challenging play with stunning natural beauty. With world-class courses spread across the islands, golfers can enjoy unforgettable rounds surrounded by lush landscapes and breathtaking ocean views. Whether you're seeking a challenging championship course or a more relaxed round with friends, Hawaii's top golf courses offer something for everyone in the ultimate golfing paradise.

# CHAPTER 7: BEST BEACHES OF HAWAII

## Waikiki Beach: The Jewel of Oahu

Waikiki Beach, located on the south shore of Oahu, is one of the most famous beaches in the world. With its golden sands, crystal-clear waters, and vibrant atmosphere, it has become a premier destination for tourists and locals alike. Historically a playground for Hawaiian royalty, Waikiki has transformed into a bustling hub of activity, offering a perfect blend of relaxation, adventure, and cultural experiences.

### 1. A Historical Overview

Once reserved for Hawaiian monarchs, Waikiki's transformation began in the late 19th century when the area was developed into a resort destination. The beach gained popularity, attracting visitors with its stunning scenery and inviting climate. Over the years, Waikiki has evolved into a lively neighborhood filled with hotels, restaurants, shops, and entertainment options, while still retaining its natural beauty and charm.

## 2. Beaches and Activities

Waikiki Beach itself stretches over two miles, offering ample space for sunbathing, swimming, and water sports. The beach is ideal for families, with gentle waves that provide a safe environment for children. Visitors can rent surfboards, paddleboards, and kayaks to explore the warm waters. Surfing is particularly popular here, with lessons available for beginners wanting to ride the iconic waves of Oahu.

Beyond water sports, Waikiki Beach is home to numerous activities and attractions. Beachfront parks, like Kapiolani Park, offer lush green spaces for picnics, jogging, and leisurely strolls. As the sun sets, the beach transforms into a vibrant hub of nightlife, with beach bars and restaurants serving delicious local cuisine and refreshing cocktails.

## 3. Cultural Experiences

Waikiki Beach is also a gateway to experiencing Hawaiian culture. Visitors can partake in traditional Hawaiian luaus, where they can enjoy hula performances, live music, and authentic island dishes. The Duke Kahanamoku Statue, honoring the legendary Hawaiian surfer and Olympic champion, is a popular landmark, symbolizing the spirit of aloha and water sports.

## 4. Shopping and Dining

The beachfront area boasts an array of shopping options, from high-end boutiques to local craft markets. The International Marketplace offers unique souvenirs and artisanal goods, making it a perfect spot to find mementos of your trip. Dining options are plentiful, ranging from casual beachfront cafes to upscale restaurants, featuring fresh seafood and local specialties.

In summary, Waikiki Beach is more than just a beautiful stretch of sand; it is a vibrant destination that offers a diverse array of activities, cultural experiences, and stunning scenery. Whether you're lounging under the sun, catching waves, or exploring local attractions, Waikiki Beach promises an unforgettable experience in the heart of Oahu, making it a must-visit for anyone traveling to Hawaii.

## Lanikai Beach: A Slice of Paradise on Oahu

Nestled on the windward coast of Oahu, Lanikai Beach is often hailed as one of the most beautiful beaches in the world. With its powdery white sand, crystal-clear turquoise waters, and stunning views of the Mokulua Islands, Lanikai offers a serene escape for both locals and visitors. Unlike the bustling atmosphere of Waikiki, Lanikai presents a more tranquil and picturesque setting, making it a perfect destination for relaxation and outdoor activities.

1. **Natural Beauty and Scenic Views**
Lanikai Beach spans approximately half a mile, framed by swaying palm trees and lush vegetation. The beach's soft sand feels like walking on flour, inviting visitors to sink their toes into its warmth. The vibrant colors of the ocean, ranging from deep blue to vibrant aqua, create a breathtaking backdrop for photography and leisurely strolls. The Mokulua Islands, located just offshore, add to the beach's charm, enticing adventurers with the promise of exploration.

2. **Water Activities and Recreation**
Lanikai Beach is a paradise for water sports enthusiasts. The calm waters are perfect for swimming, paddleboarding, and kayaking, with rentals available nearby. Many visitors take the opportunity to kayak to the Mokulua Islands, where they can explore hidden beaches and snorkeling spots teeming with marine life.

Snorkeling off the beach also reveals a colorful underwater world, with tropical fish and vibrant coral reefs waiting to be discovered.

### 3. **Sunrise and Sunset Views**

One of the beach's most magical experiences is witnessing the sunrise. Lanikai Beach faces east, making it an ideal spot to watch the daybreak over the horizon. As the sun rises, the sky transforms into a canvas of oranges, pinks, and yellows, reflecting beautifully on the water. Sunset, though not as famous as sunrise, offers equally stunning views as the sky lights up with soft hues, making for a perfect romantic setting.

### 4. **Community and Culture**

Lanikai Beach is located near the charming community of Kailua, which offers an array of local shops, cafes, and restaurants. Visitors can explore the nearby Lanikai neighborhood, known for its picturesque homes and friendly atmosphere. The area embodies the spirit of aloha, welcoming everyone to enjoy the beauty of Hawaii.

In conclusion, Lanikai Beach is a true gem of Oahu, offering visitors an idyllic setting to unwind and connect with nature. With its stunning natural beauty, array of water activities, and peaceful ambiance, it's no wonder that Lanikai Beach is a favorite destination for those seeking a slice of paradise. Whether you're looking to relax in the sun, embark on an adventure, or simply soak in the breathtaking views, Lanikai Beach promises an unforgettable experience in Hawaii.

## Ka'anapali Beach: A Maui Gem

Ka'anapali Beach, located on the northwest shore of Maui, is a breathtaking stretch of golden sand and azure waters that epitomizes the beauty of Hawaii. Once the playground of Hawaiian royalty, Ka'anapali has evolved into a premier resort destination, attracting visitors from around the world with its stunning scenery, luxurious accommodations, and vibrant atmosphere.

1. **Natural Beauty and Scenic Landscapes**

Spanning approximately three miles, Ka'anapali Beach is renowned for its picturesque views of the neighboring island of Lanai and the stunning sunsets that paint the sky with vibrant hues. The beach is framed by lush tropical vegetation and the iconic Black Rock, a lava formation that serves as a popular spot for snorkeling and diving. The calm, clear waters are perfect for swimming and water sports, making it a favorite among families and adventure seekers alike.

2. **Water Activities and Adventures**

Ka'anapali Beach offers an array of water activities for visitors to enjoy. Snorkeling at Black Rock is a highlight, where snorkelers can encounter colorful fish, sea turtles, and even the occasional reef shark. For those seeking more adrenaline, paddleboarding and kayaking provide opportunities to explore the coastline and nearby coves. Additionally, boat tours and whale watching excursions are popular during the winter months, offering a chance to see humpback whales in their natural habitat.

## 3. Resorts and Amenities
The beach is lined with world-class resorts, offering luxurious accommodations and amenities. Visitors can indulge in spa treatments, fine dining, and various entertainment options without ever leaving the beachfront. The Ka'anapali Beach Walk, a scenic path that runs parallel to the beach, is perfect for a leisurely stroll, providing access to shops, restaurants, and cultural experiences.

## 4. Cultural Experiences and Events
Ka'anapali Beach is also a hub for Hawaiian culture. Visitors can attend traditional luaus, where they can savor local cuisine while enjoying hula performances and live music. The beach hosts events throughout the year, including the popular "Tropical Gardens of Maui" and sunset ceremonies, allowing visitors to immerse themselves in the rich culture of the islands.

In conclusion, Ka'anapali Beach is a true Maui gem that offers a perfect blend of natural beauty, adventure, and luxury. Whether you're relaxing on the soft sands, exploring the vibrant underwater world, or indulging in the local culture, Ka'anapali promises an unforgettable Hawaiian experience. With its stunning scenery and abundance of activities, it's no wonder that this iconic beach remains a top destination for travelers seeking the quintessential Hawaiian getaway.

## *Hapuna Beach: A Pristine Paradise on the Big Island*

Hapuna Beach, located on the Big Island of Hawaii, is celebrated for its stunning natural beauty and pristine white sands. Nestled along the western coast, this beach is often regarded as one of the best in Hawaii, attracting both locals and tourists seeking a picturesque spot to relax and enjoy the sun. With its expansive shoreline and crystal-clear waters, Hapuna Beach offers a perfect blend of adventure and tranquility, making it an ideal destination for beachgoers of all ages.

## 1. Natural Beauty and Scenic Landscapes

Hapuna Beach stretches approximately half a mile, boasting soft white sand and azure waters that are perfect for swimming and sunbathing. The beach is framed by lush green hills and volcanic landscapes, providing a striking contrast to the vibrant blue of the ocean. The clear waters are not only inviting for swimming but also excellent for snorkeling, allowing visitors to explore the rich marine life that thrives in the coral reefs nearby.

## 2. Water Activities and Recreation

Water activities abound at Hapuna Beach. Swimming is popular here, especially during the summer months when the waves are gentler. Lifeguards are on duty, ensuring a safe environment for families and children. For those looking for adventure, snorkeling gear can be rented nearby, providing an opportunity to discover colorful fish and marine creatures in their natural habitat. Stand-up paddleboarding and bodyboarding are also favorite pastimes at this stunning beach.

### 3. Amenities and Accessibility

Hapuna Beach State Park provides ample amenities for visitors, including restrooms, showers, and picnic areas, making it easy to spend a full day at the beach. Ample parking is available, and the park's well-maintained facilities ensure a comfortable experience for all. The park's serene atmosphere and well-kept grounds encourage relaxation, allowing visitors to soak in the beauty of their surroundings.

### 4. Sunset Views and Relaxation

One of the most magical experiences at Hapuna Beach is watching the sunset. As the sun dips below the horizon, the sky transforms into a canvas of oranges, pinks, and purples, casting a warm glow over the beach. This breathtaking view makes for a perfect romantic setting or a serene moment for reflection, enhancing the beach's allure.

In conclusion, Hapuna Beach is a true treasure of the Big Island, offering visitors an idyllic escape filled with sun, sand, and stunning scenery. Whether you're seeking adventure through water sports or simply looking to relax under the Hawaiian sun, Hapuna Beach provides a perfect setting to create unforgettable memories in paradise. Its natural beauty and tranquil atmosphere make it a must-visit destination for anyone exploring the Big Island of Hawaii.

## Hanalei Bay: A Jewel of Kauai

Nestled on the north shore of Kauai, Hanalei Bay is a stunning crescent-shaped beach renowned for its breathtaking scenery and serene atmosphere. With emerald mountains rising dramatically in the background and lush taro fields dotting the landscape, Hanalei Bay is often considered one of the most picturesque locations in Hawaii. This tranquil bay offers a perfect blend of natural beauty, outdoor activities, and rich cultural experiences, making it a must-visit destination for travelers.

1. **Natural Beauty and Scenic Landscapes**

Hanalei Bay is characterized by its striking vistas, where the azure waters of the Pacific Ocean meet golden sands. The beach stretches for over two miles, providing ample space for sunbathing, swimming, and beachcombing. The dramatic cliffs and waterfalls in the surrounding mountains create a breathtaking backdrop, especially during the rainy season when the waterfalls cascade down the verdant slopes. The bay is also famous for its sunsets, with vibrant colors illuminating the sky as the sun sets over the horizon, providing an idyllic setting for romantic evenings.

2. **Water Activities and Adventures**

Hanalei Bay is a haven for water enthusiasts. The calm waters during the summer months are perfect for swimming, kayaking, and paddleboarding, allowing visitors to explore the bay's beauty from the water. Snorkeling is another popular activity, with colorful fish and vibrant coral reefs waiting to be discovered in the shallower areas. During the winter months, the surf picks up, attracting experienced surfers who come to ride the powerful waves that roll into the bay.

3. **Cultural Experiences and Community**
The charming town of Hanalei is just a short walk from the beach, where visitors can experience the local culture and community. The town features a variety of shops, art galleries, and restaurants serving delicious Hawaiian cuisine, including fresh poke and traditional plate lunches. The Hanalei National Wildlife Refuge, located nearby, offers opportunities for birdwatching and appreciating the unique flora and fauna of the region.

In conclusion, Hanalei Bay is a true gem of Kauai, offering visitors an unforgettable experience filled with natural beauty, outdoor adventures, and cultural richness. Whether you're lounging on the beach, exploring the vibrant underwater world, or enjoying the local cuisine in the town, Hanalei Bay promises a perfect escape into paradise. Its stunning landscapes and welcoming atmosphere make it a must-visit destination for anyone traveling to Hawaii.

# CHAPTER 8: HAWAIIAN CUISINE AND DINING

## Traditional Hawaiian Foods: Poi, Poke, and More

Hawaiian cuisine is a vibrant tapestry of flavors, influenced by the islands' diverse cultures and rich agricultural resources. Traditional Hawaiian foods are deeply rooted in the islands' history, reflecting the indigenous practices of the Native Hawaiians as well as the contributions of immigrants from Asia, Europe, and the Americas. Here's a closer look at some iconic Hawaiian dishes, including poi, poke, and other culinary delights that embody the essence of Hawaiian culture.

### 1. **Poi: The Staple of Hawaiian Diet**
Poi is perhaps the most quintessential Hawaiian food. Made from the taro root, poi is a staple

starch that has been consumed by Native Hawaiians for centuries. The process begins with steaming or baking the taro, which is then pounded into a smooth, sticky paste. Poi is often served as a side dish and has a mildly tangy flavor that pairs well with savory meats and fish. Traditionally, it is eaten with the fingers, making it a communal dish that brings people together during family gatherings and luaus.

## 2. Poke: A Fresh Taste of the Sea

Poke, meaning "to slice" in Hawaiian, is a popular dish that showcases the islands' abundant seafood. Typically made with fresh, raw fish like ahi (yellowfin tuna) or octopus, poke is seasoned with ingredients such as soy sauce, sesame oil, seaweed, and onions. Each poke bowl reflects local flavors and can be customized with a variety of toppings, making it a favorite for both locals and visitors. Poke is not only a delicious and refreshing dish but also a testament to Hawaii's deep connection to the ocean.

## 3. Loco Moco: A Comfort Food Favorite

Loco moco is a beloved comfort food that has become a staple in Hawaiian diners. This hearty dish consists of a bed of rice topped with a hamburger patty, a sunny-side-up egg, and a generous drizzle of brown gravy. The combination of flavors and textures makes loco moco a filling and satisfying meal, often enjoyed for breakfast or lunch. Variations can include additional toppings such as sautéed mushrooms or macaroni salad, showcasing the flexibility and creativity of Hawaiian cuisine.

## 4. Other Notable Dishes

Other traditional Hawaiian foods include kalua pig, which is slow-cooked in an underground oven called an imu, resulting in tender, smoky meat; laulau, which features pork and fish wrapped in taro leaves and steamed; and haupia, a coconut milk-based dessert served as a pudding or pie filling. Each dish tells a story and reflects the unique culinary heritage of the islands.

In conclusion, traditional Hawaiian foods are more than just meals; they are a celebration of culture, community, and history. From the staple poi to the refreshing poke and hearty loco moco, these dishes offer a delicious way to experience the rich flavors and traditions of Hawaii. For anyone visiting the islands, indulging in these culinary delights is essential to understanding and appreciating the vibrant Hawaiian way of life.

## Best Luau Experiences in Hawaii

A luau is one of the most iconic and culturally rich experiences you can have while visiting Hawaii. These vibrant celebrations showcase the islands' traditional music, hula dancing, and delicious cuisine, providing guests with a unique glimpse into Hawaiian culture and hospitality. From the lively performances to the mouthwatering feast, here are some of the best luau experiences across the Hawaiian Islands that promise an unforgettable evening.

## 1. **Old Lahaina Luau (Maui)**

Old Lahaina Luau is often regarded as one of the most authentic luaus on the islands. Set on the beautiful beachfront in Lahaina, this luau offers a stunning sunset view while guests are treated to traditional Hawaiian entertainment. The evening begins with a ceremonial unearthing of the pig, which has been slow-roasted in an imu (underground oven). Guests can enjoy a buffet featuring local favorites such as poi, kalua pig, and fresh fish, all while watching talented performers share the history and stories of Hawaii through song and dance.

## 2. **Smith's Tropical Paradise Luau (Kauai)**

Situated in the lush setting of Wailua, Smith's Tropical Paradise Luau combines breathtaking scenery with a rich cultural experience. Guests can stroll through beautiful gardens before enjoying a buffet-style dinner featuring local cuisine. The evening's entertainment includes a blend of traditional Hawaiian hula, Tahitian dance, and fire-knife performances. This luau also provides an interactive element, allowing guests to participate in traditional crafts and games, making it a fantastic option for families.

### 3. Feast at Lele (Maui)

For a more intimate and upscale luau experience, the Feast at Lele in Lahaina offers a unique twist. Unlike traditional luaus, where food is served buffet-style, this dining experience features a multi-course meal served directly to your table. Each course represents different regions of Polynesia, accompanied by live music and performances that showcase the culture of each area. The setting is romantic and picturesque, with an oceanfront view that enhances the overall experience.

### 4. Paradise Cove Luau (Oahu)

Paradise Cove Luau, located in Ko Olina on Oahu, is one of the largest and most popular luaus in Hawaii. The event begins with a variety of activities, such as lei-making, hula lessons, and coconut tree climbing. Guests can enjoy a delicious buffet dinner featuring a wide selection of Hawaiian dishes before the evening culminates in an impressive stage show that tells the story of Hawaiian culture through vibrant dance and music.

In conclusion, attending a luau is a must-do experience for anyone visiting Hawaii. Each of these luaus offers a unique way to immerse yourself in the rich culture and traditions of the islands while enjoying delicious food and captivating entertainment. Whether you're looking for authenticity, a family-friendly atmosphere, or an upscale dining experience, the diverse luaus across Hawaii promise a memorable night filled with laughter, music, and a taste of paradise.

## *Farm-to-Table: Local and Sustainable Dining in Hawaii*

Hawaii's unique geographic location and diverse ecosystems provide an abundance of fresh, locally sourced ingredients, making it an ideal place for farm-to-table dining. This movement, which emphasizes the importance of sustainability and supporting local agriculture, is becoming increasingly popular across the islands. By focusing on seasonal ingredients and reducing the distance food travels from farm to plate, Hawaii's restaurants are not only offering delicious meals but also contributing to the preservation of the islands' rich agricultural heritage.

## 1. The Importance of Local Sourcing

Hawaii's agriculture is as diverse as its culture, producing everything from tropical fruits and vegetables to grass-fed beef and sustainable seafood. Many local farms specialize in organic practices, ensuring that the produce is not only fresh but also free of harmful chemicals. By sourcing ingredients from nearby farms, restaurants can offer menus that reflect the islands' bounty while also supporting local farmers and the economy. This connection fosters a sense of community and sustainability, promoting environmental responsibility.

## 2. **Culinary Innovation and Creativity**

Hawaii's farm-to-table dining scene is characterized by culinary innovation, where chefs creatively incorporate local ingredients into traditional Hawaiian dishes and modern cuisine. Restaurants often change their menus based on seasonal availability, highlighting the freshest produce and seafood. This approach allows diners to experience the true flavors of Hawaii, such as ripe mangoes, sweet taro, and fresh fish caught the same day. Signature dishes may include poke made with locally sourced fish, lilikoi (passion fruit) drizzles over desserts, or salads featuring greens and vegetables grown just miles away.

## 3. **Dining Experiences Across the Islands**

Various restaurants across the Hawaiian Islands embrace the farm-to-table philosophy. For example, Merriman's in Maui is known for its commitment to local sourcing, offering dishes that highlight the region's freshest ingredients. On the Big Island, Hilo's Farm to Table restaurant features a menu focused on organic produce and sustainable proteins. Meanwhile, Kona Brewing Company not only brews its craft beers using local ingredients but also supports local farmers by sourcing produce for its dishes.

4. **Sustainability and Community Impact**

In addition to serving delicious food, farm-to-table restaurants contribute to environmental sustainability by reducing carbon footprints associated with food transportation. Many establishments also engage in practices like composting and recycling, further enhancing their commitment to the environment. By promoting local agriculture and sustainable dining, these restaurants play a vital role in educating the community about the importance of eating locally and supporting Hawaiian culture.

In conclusion, the farm-to-table movement in Hawaii is more than just a dining trend; it's a celebration of local agriculture, sustainability, and culinary creativity. By prioritizing fresh, locally sourced ingredients, restaurants across the islands are crafting unforgettable dining experiences while fostering a deeper connection to the land and its people. Whether you're enjoying a meal with ocean views or in a charming farm setting, embracing farm-to-table dining in Hawaii allows you to savor the islands' flavors while supporting the local community and environment.

## Popular Local Eateries and Fine Dining in Hawaii

Hawaii's culinary landscape is a vibrant tapestry woven from diverse cultural influences, rich local ingredients, and time-honored traditions. From casual eateries serving mouthwatering local fare to upscale restaurants offering fine dining experiences, the islands present a culinary journey that reflects their unique heritage and natural abundance. Here are some popular local eateries and fine dining establishments that showcase the best of Hawaiian cuisine.

## 1. **Local Eateries: The Heart of Hawaiian Cuisine**

**Aloha Mixed Plate (Maui)**
Located in Lahaina, Aloha Mixed Plate is a beloved local eatery known for its authentic Hawaiian plate lunches. The menu features generous portions of kalua pig, lomi lomi salmon, and mac salad, all served with steamed rice. Diners can enjoy their meals with a breathtaking view of the ocean, making it a perfect spot for a casual lunch.

**Ono Seafood (Oahu)**
Famous for its poke, Ono Seafood is a must-visit for seafood lovers in Honolulu. This local gem offers an array of poke varieties, including spicy tuna and traditional shoyu poke. The fresh,

high-quality fish, combined with delicious marinades, makes it a go-to spot for locals and tourists alike seeking an authentic taste of Hawaii.

**Rainbow Drive-In (Oahu)**
A staple in the local dining scene, Rainbow Drive-In serves classic Hawaiian comfort food. From its famous loco moco to refreshing shave ice, this casual diner is perfect for those looking to indulge in hearty, satisfying meals. The friendly atmosphere and affordable prices make it a favorite among families and visitors.

## 2. Fine Dining: Elevating Hawaiian Cuisine

**Mama's Fish House (Maui)**
Renowned for its breathtaking beachfront location, Mama's Fish House offers an upscale dining experience featuring the freshest seafood. The menu highlights locally caught fish, expertly prepared and paired with tropical flavors. The ambiance, complete with traditional Hawaiian

decor and stunning ocean views, makes it a romantic setting for a memorable dinner.

**Chef Mavro (Oahu)**
For a truly unique fine dining experience, Chef Mavro in Honolulu combines French culinary techniques with Hawaiian ingredients. Chef George Mavrothalassitis crafts exquisite dishes that reflect the islands' flavors, featuring locally sourced produce and seafood. The intimate setting and exceptional service elevate the dining experience, making it ideal for special occasions.

**Hau Tree Lanai (Oahu)**
Set in a historic beachside location, Hau Tree Lanai offers a sophisticated yet relaxed dining experience. The menu features a fusion of local and international flavors, with an emphasis on fresh, seasonal ingredients. Guests can enjoy their meals under a large hau tree, overlooking the ocean, creating a picturesque backdrop for any dining occasion.

In conclusion, Hawaii's culinary scene is a delightful blend of local eateries and fine dining establishments that cater to all tastes and budgets. Whether you're craving a casual plate lunch or an exquisite fine dining experience, the islands offer an array of options that highlight the rich flavors and cultural heritage of Hawaiian cuisine. Exploring these popular spots not only satisfies your palate but also deepens your appreciation for the islands' culinary traditions and the passionate chefs who bring them to life.

## *Farmers Markets and Food Trucks: A Taste of Local Flavor in Hawaii*

Hawaii's culinary scene is vibrant and diverse, showcasing the islands' rich agricultural heritage and the creativity of its chefs. Among the best ways to experience this unique culinary culture are farmers markets and food trucks. Both provide locals and visitors alike with fresh, locally sourced ingredients and delicious meals that reflect Hawaii's diverse flavors and influences.

## 1. Farmers Markets: Freshness and Community

Farmers markets are essential to Hawaii's food culture, connecting local farmers and artisans directly with consumers. These markets offer an array of fresh produce, including tropical fruits like pineapples, mangoes, and papayas, alongside locally grown vegetables such as taro, sweet potatoes, and leafy greens. Each island hosts its own farmers markets, with notable ones like the Kapiolani Community College Farmers Market on Oahu and the Maui County Farmers Market.

Visiting a farmers market is more than just shopping; it's an immersive experience. Shoppers can meet the farmers, learn about their growing practices, and even participate in cooking demonstrations. Many markets also feature local artisans selling handmade crafts, baked goods, and gourmet products like honey and jams. The atmosphere is vibrant, filled with the sounds of live music and the scents of freshly prepared food, making it an enjoyable outing for families and friends.

2. **Food Trucks: A Culinary Adventure on Wheels**
Hawaii's food truck scene has exploded in recent years, offering a diverse range of cuisines that reflect the multicultural influences of the islands. From traditional Hawaiian dishes to international flavors, food trucks provide convenient and delicious meals at affordable prices. Popular food trucks, such as Giovanni's Shrimp Truck on Oahu, are famous for their garlic shrimp plates, while Maui's Da Poke Shack serves some of the freshest poke on the island.

Food trucks often set up in bustling areas, allowing diners to enjoy their meals outdoors. Many food trucks have developed a loyal following, and their menus frequently change based on seasonal ingredients and local availability. This dynamic nature allows for culinary experimentation, making each visit a new adventure in flavor.

### 3. Supporting Local Economies

Both farmers markets and food trucks play a significant role in supporting Hawaii's local economy. By purchasing from local farmers and artisans, consumers contribute to sustainable agricultural practices and help preserve Hawaii's agricultural landscape. Additionally, food trucks provide opportunities for aspiring chefs and entrepreneurs to share their culinary creations without the overhead costs of a traditional restaurant.

In conclusion, farmers markets and food trucks are integral to the culinary experience in Hawaii, offering fresh, locally sourced ingredients and a diverse array of flavors. These vibrant venues not only promote community and sustainability but also allow visitors to connect with the islands' rich agricultural traditions. Whether you're browsing the stalls at a farmers market or savoring a meal from a food truck, you'll discover the heart and soul of Hawaiian cuisine, making for an unforgettable experience.

# CHAPTER 9: ACCOMMODATIONS: WHERE TO STAY

## Luxury Resorts and Beachfront Hotels in Hawaii

Hawaii's tropical landscapes, stunning beaches, and vibrant culture have made it one of the world's top luxury travel destinations. The islands are home to some of the finest luxury resorts and beachfront hotels, offering an unparalleled combination of natural beauty, high-end accommodations, and world-class amenities. Whether you seek a romantic getaway, a family vacation, or a serene retreat, Hawaii's luxury resorts provide a perfect blend of relaxation, adventure, and indulgence.

**1. Oahu: Glamour Meets Tradition**

Oahu, known as "The Gathering Place," offers a wide variety of luxury accommodations, from iconic beachfront hotels to secluded resorts. The Royal Hawaiian, located on the famous Waikiki Beach, is one of the most recognizable luxury hotels in Hawaii. Known as "The Pink Palace of the Pacific," this historic resort offers oceanfront rooms, elegant dining, and a tranquil ambiance, blending classic Hawaiian style with modern comforts. Halekulani, another Oahu gem, provides a serene escape with unobstructed views of Diamond Head and five-star service, featuring luxurious spa treatments and fine dining at its renowned restaurant, La Mer.

For travelers looking for a more secluded experience, The Kahala Hotel & Resort, just a short drive from Waikiki, offers exclusivity with its private beach and lagoon filled with dolphins. This luxury resort is known for its sophisticated service, gourmet dining, and a peaceful setting away from the hustle and bustle of the city.

2. **Maui: Paradise and Adventure**

Maui is home to some of Hawaii's most prestigious resorts, particularly along its beautiful Ka'anapali and Wailea coastlines. The Four Seasons Resort Maui at Wailea is a standout, offering spacious suites, an infinity pool, and personalized service. With its beachfront location, this resort offers activities such as snorkeling, golfing, and whale watching, in addition to a world-class spa.

For a family-friendly yet luxurious experience, The Ritz-Carlton Kapalua is nestled amidst lush greenery on Maui's northwestern shore. This resort combines luxury with adventure, providing access to hiking trails, championship golf courses, and traditional Hawaiian cultural programs.

### 3. Big Island: Luxury Amid Volcanoes

On the Big Island, visitors can enjoy both luxury and dramatic landscapes. The Four Seasons Resort Hualalai offers an extraordinary combination of elegant accommodations and direct access to the rugged beauty of Hawaii's volcanic coast. With its open-air design, beachfront bungalows, and private golf course, Hualalai exemplifies the natural luxury that the Big Island offers. The resort also boasts a renowned spa and several restaurants serving locally sourced cuisine.

4. **Kauai: Seclusion and Natural Beauty**
Kauai's unspoiled landscapes make it a haven for luxury resorts that emphasize privacy and natural beauty. The St. Regis Princeville Resort, located on the island's north shore, offers dramatic views of Hanalei Bay and the Na Pali Coast. Known for its luxurious rooms, infinity pool, and personalized service, this resort is ideal for honeymooners and those seeking tranquility.

Grand Hyatt Kauai Resort and Spa, located on the island's southern shore, is another favorite, offering lush gardens, river pools, and a top-rated spa, blending the resort's luxury with Kauai's laid-back atmosphere.

Hawaii's luxury resorts and beachfront hotels offer the ultimate escape, providing guests with an extraordinary mix of natural beauty, first-class service, and diverse activities. Whether staying in a historic hotel in Waikiki, a five-star resort on Maui's sunny shores, or a secluded retreat on Kauai or the Big Island, these resorts create unforgettable experiences that showcase the very best of Hawaiian hospitality and scenery. For those seeking luxury in paradise, Hawaii's top resorts offer a perfect balance of relaxation, adventure, and indulgence.

## Vacation Rentals and Boutique Inns in Hawaii

For travelers seeking a more personalized and intimate experience in Hawaii, vacation rentals and boutique inns offer an appealing alternative to the traditional luxury resort scene. These accommodations provide a unique opportunity to connect with the islands' culture and lifestyle, often located in more secluded or residential areas. Whether you're looking for a private beachside retreat, a cozy bungalow in the mountains, or a charming inn with local flair, Hawaii's vacation rentals and boutique inns cater to a wide range of preferences and budgets.

## 1. Vacation Rentals: A Home Away From Home

Vacation rentals in Hawaii are popular among visitors who want the flexibility and privacy of having their own space. These rentals range from beachfront villas and oceanfront condos to rustic cabins and cozy cottages tucked away in the lush Hawaiian countryside. Platforms like Airbnb, Vrbo, and local rental agencies offer a wide selection, allowing guests to find properties that fit their style and needs.

For those traveling with family or in groups, vacation rentals provide space and comfort that many hotels or resorts may not. With amenities like fully equipped kitchens, multiple bedrooms, and outdoor areas with BBQ grills or private pools, guests can enjoy home-cooked meals, host gatherings, or simply relax in a setting that feels like a home away from home.

Popular destinations for vacation rentals include beachfront homes in Wailea (Maui), private estates on the North Shore of Oahu, and charming cottages on the Big Island's Kona Coast. These rentals often allow travelers to explore less touristy areas, offering a more authentic Hawaiian experience.

**2. Boutique Inns: Charm and Local Flavor**
Boutique inns in Hawaii are smaller, independently owned properties that offer a unique blend of local hospitality, charm, and personalized service. Many boutique inns emphasize the surrounding natural beauty, with scenic views of the ocean, mountains, or tropical gardens. These inns often have fewer rooms than large resorts, which fosters a more intimate and cozy atmosphere for guests.

The Surfjack Hotel & Swim Club in Waikiki (Oahu) is an example of a boutique hotel that combines mid-century modern design with laid-back Hawaiian vibes. Its retro aesthetic, combined with a lively social scene around its iconic pool, makes it a favorite for visitors looking for something different.

On Maui, The Plantation Inn offers an intimate bed-and-breakfast experience in the heart of Lahaina, with charming plantation-style architecture and a tranquil setting. Guests can enjoy a gourmet breakfast, as well as access to the amenities of its sister property, The Kaanapali Beach Hotel.

### 3. Why Choose Vacation Rentals or Boutique Inns?

Choosing a vacation rental or boutique inn allows for more privacy, independence, and often, a deeper connection to the local community. These accommodations tend to be more immersive, offering insights into the local culture and lifestyle, with many located in residential neighborhoods or off-the-beaten-path locations. Additionally, vacation rentals and boutique inns provide opportunities to explore the islands at your own pace and avoid the crowds often found at larger resorts.

Hawaii's vacation rentals and boutique inns offer a perfect alternative for travelers looking for a more personalized and authentic experience. Whether it's a private villa with ocean views, a mountain hideaway, or a charming inn filled with local charm, these accommodations provide the flexibility and intimacy that larger hotels often cannot. For those who want to immerse themselves in the natural beauty and culture of Hawaii, staying in a vacation rental or boutique inn can create unforgettable memories of island life.

## Budget-Friendly Hostels and Camping in Hawaii

Hawaii is often associated with luxury resorts and high-end accommodations, but for budget-conscious travelers, there are plenty of affordable options that allow you to experience the islands without breaking the bank. Budget-friendly hostels and camping spots offer a unique way to explore Hawaii's stunning landscapes, rich culture, and outdoor adventures while keeping expenses low. Whether you're a solo traveler, backpacker, or an outdoor enthusiast, Hawaii has a variety of economical lodging options that still provide a memorable experience.

1. **Hostels: Affordable and Social**
Hawaii's hostels are ideal for budget travelers seeking affordable accommodations and a chance to meet fellow adventurers. Hostels offer dorm-style rooms with shared facilities, and some even have private rooms available at a lower cost than hotels. In addition to saving on lodging, many hostels provide communal kitchens, allowing guests to prepare their own meals and save on dining costs.

One of the most popular hostels is The Beach Waikiki Boutique Hostel in Honolulu (Oahu), located just a short walk from Waikiki Beach. The hostel offers a mix of dorms and private rooms, free breakfast, and rooftop BBQ nights. Its prime location and friendly atmosphere make it a great spot for travelers looking to explore Oahu's top attractions while on a budget.

In Maui, The Northshore Hostel in Wailuku offers budget-friendly accommodations near hiking trails, beaches, and local attractions. The hostel emphasizes a community feel, with shared kitchens, free Wi-Fi, and organized social events, making it easy for travelers to connect with others.

For an eco-friendly option, The Big Island Hostel in Hilo offers clean, comfortable accommodations and promotes sustainable travel practices. Located near Hawaii Volcanoes National Park, it's perfect for those looking to explore the Big Island's natural wonders.

## 2. Camping: Immersive and Cost-Effective

Camping in Hawaii offers an immersive experience for outdoor enthusiasts who want to be surrounded by the islands' natural beauty. There are numerous campgrounds across the islands, located in state parks, national parks, and even on beachfront properties. Camping is not only budget-friendly but also provides a closer connection to Hawaii's landscapes, from tropical rainforests and volcanic craters to sandy beaches and coastal cliffs.

On Oahu, Malaekahana Beach Campground offers beachside camping with basic amenities, such as showers and restrooms, making it a popular spot for campers who want easy access to the ocean. For a more rugged experience, Kalalau Beach on Kauai's Na Pali Coast requires a challenging hike to reach but rewards visitors with one of the most remote and beautiful camping spots in Hawaii.

Volcanoes National Park on the Big Island also offers campsites, allowing campers to explore the park's volcanic landscapes, craters, and lava tubes up close. Many of the campgrounds are situated near trails, making it easy for visitors to hike and explore during their stay.

3. **Permits and Planning**

For those interested in camping, it's important to note that many campsites in Hawaii require permits, which should be obtained in advance. Availability can be limited during peak seasons, so early planning is recommended. Additionally, campers should be aware of the local regulations and pack accordingly, as some campgrounds have limited amenities, and Hawaii's weather can change quickly.

Budget-friendly hostels and camping options in Hawaii offer a fantastic way to explore the islands without spending a fortune. Hostels provide affordable accommodations with the added benefit of social interaction, while camping offers an immersive, nature-filled experience. Whether you're lounging in a beachside hammock, exploring volcanic landscapes, or meeting fellow travelers at a hostel, these budget options ensure that Hawaii's beauty and adventure are accessible to all.

## Eco-Friendly Stays: Sustainable Accommodation Options in Hawaii

As travelers become more conscious of their environmental impact, eco-friendly accommodations in Hawaii have gained popularity. From sustainable resorts to green-certified hotels and eco-lodges, the islands offer numerous options for those seeking to minimize their carbon footprint while enjoying the natural beauty of Hawaii. These accommodations focus on sustainable practices such as using renewable energy, sourcing local products, reducing waste, and promoting environmental conservation. By choosing eco-friendly stays, visitors not only support local communities but also contribute to the preservation of Hawaii's fragile ecosystems.

**1. Eco-Lodges: Immersed in Nature**
Eco-lodges in Hawaii are designed to offer an immersive, low-impact experience that connects guests with the environment. Typically located in more remote areas, these lodges emphasize sustainability through eco-conscious architecture, organic farming, and energy-efficient practices. Many eco-lodges operate on solar power, recycle waste, and grow their own produce to reduce their environmental impact.

On the Big Island, Volcano Eco Retreat is a prime example of an eco-lodge that focuses on sustainability. Nestled in a lush rainforest near Hawaii Volcanoes National Park, the retreat is entirely off-grid, powered by solar energy and designed with minimal environmental impact in mind. Guests can enjoy organic, locally sourced meals and eco-conscious amenities, all while experiencing the natural beauty of the surrounding landscape.

In Maui, The Hana Tropicals Farm Stay offers a more rustic, sustainable experience. This eco-lodge focuses on regenerative farming practices, allowing guests to stay on an active tropical farm while enjoying the island's unspoiled nature.

2. **Sustainable Resorts and Green Hotels**

Several resorts and hotels in Hawaii are adopting green practices, aiming to reduce their environmental footprint without compromising luxury and comfort. The Fairmont Orchid on the Big Island, for instance, is certified by the Hawaii Green Business Program. This resort incorporates sustainability into its daily operations by conserving water, using energy-efficient systems, and supporting local farmers through farm-to-table dining.

The Westin Nanea Ocean Villas in Maui is another example of a resort that promotes sustainable living. With a commitment to energy efficiency, waste reduction, and water conservation, the Westin Nanea incorporates green practices while providing guests with luxury villas and access to the island's natural beauty. The resort also educates guests on local culture and sustainability through various programs and activities.

## 3. **Farm Stays: Sustainable Agriculture and Tourism**

Farm stays provide a unique opportunity to stay on working farms that practice sustainable agriculture. Guests can experience firsthand how local farmers grow organic produce, raise animals, and support the local economy. On the Big Island, Kahua Ranch offers an immersive farm stay experience where guests can learn about sustainable ranching, hike through pastures, and enjoy farm-fresh meals.

These farm stays offer a deeper connection to the land and provide guests with insights into the importance of sustainable agriculture in maintaining Hawaii's ecosystems.

## 4. **Supporting Local Communities**

Choosing eco-friendly accommodations in Hawaii not only helps the environment but also supports local communities. Many eco-friendly stays are locally owned and employ sustainable tourism practices that promote the well-being of the islands' residents. These businesses prioritize sourcing local goods and services, thereby reducing the carbon footprint associated with imports and boosting the local economy.

Eco-friendly stays in Hawaii provide a responsible and rewarding way to experience the islands' natural beauty. From off-grid eco-lodges nestled in rainforests to green-certified resorts and sustainable farm stays, these accommodations offer a wide range of environmentally conscious options. By choosing to stay at these sustainable accommodations, travelers help preserve Hawaii's unique ecosystems, support local communities, and contribute to the long-term health of the islands.

## Family-Friendly Hotels and Resorts in Hawaii

Hawaii is a dream destination for families, offering a wide variety of accommodations that cater to all ages. Family-friendly hotels and resorts in the islands combine relaxation for parents with fun and engaging activities for children. With spacious rooms, kid-friendly amenities, and thoughtful programs, these accommodations ensure that the entire family can enjoy an unforgettable Hawaiian vacation.

### 1. Oahu: Excitement and Convenience

Oahu offers numerous family-friendly hotels, particularly around Waikiki and Ko Olina, where convenience and entertainment options are plentiful. One of the most iconic choices is Aulani, A Disney Resort & Spa in Ko Olina.

Designed with families in mind, Aulani features Disney magic infused with Hawaiian culture. It offers a lazy river, water slides, a children's pool, and a private beach lagoon, while character meet-and-greets, cultural workshops, and kid-friendly dining keep children engaged. Parents can relax at the Laniwai Spa or enjoy a romantic dinner while their kids are entertained at Aunty's Beach House, the resort's supervised kids' club.

In Waikiki, Hilton Hawaiian Village is another excellent choice for families. This expansive resort includes multiple pools, including a kid-friendly lagoon and water slides, as well as family-friendly dining options. The Camp Penguin kids' program offers activities such as lei making, hula lessons, and day trips around the island, ensuring that children have plenty of fun while parents unwind on the beach or at the spa.

## 2. Maui: Nature and Adventure

Maui is a top destination for families who want to explore the island's natural beauty while staying in comfort. The Grand Wailea, A Waldorf Astoria Resort, is a luxurious yet family-friendly option. The resort's Wailea Canyon Activity Pool features nine pools, a lazy river, and water slides, making it a paradise for children. The resort also offers the Rocky's Kids Club, a program designed to engage kids in educational and fun activities such as storytelling, arts and crafts, and games.

For a more relaxed and intimate family experience, The Westin Ka'anapali Ocean Resort Villas offers spacious villa-style accommodations with full kitchens, perfect for families who prefer to prepare their own meals. The resort's beachfront location, along with activities such as snorkeling, paddleboarding, and whale watching, ensures that the whole family will have plenty to do.

### 3. Big Island: Adventure and Education

On the Big Island, family-friendly resorts provide opportunities to explore Hawaii's volcanic landscapes, lush forests, and marine life. The Fairmont Orchid is an excellent choice for families, offering spacious rooms and suites as well as activities such as turtle-watching, snorkeling, and cultural programs. The resort's Keiki Aloha program introduces children to Hawaiian culture through hula lessons, arts and crafts, and storytelling.

For families interested in astronomy, Mauna Kea Beach Hotel offers stargazing programs that take advantage of the island's clear skies and proximity to Mauna Kea, one of the best places for stargazing in the world. This beachfront resort also provides kid-friendly dining, tennis lessons, and easy access to one of the island's most beautiful beaches.

## 4. Kauai: Serenity and Exploration

Kauai, known for its laid-back vibe and stunning natural scenery, offers family-friendly accommodations that focus on outdoor activities and relaxation. The Grand Hyatt Kauai Resort & Spa is one of the island's premier family resorts, offering a massive pool complex with a lazy river, water slides, and a saltwater lagoon. The Camp Hyatt program keeps children entertained with Hawaiian crafts, lei making, and nature walks, allowing parents to enjoy the resort's spa or golf course.

For families who prefer a more eco-friendly and adventurous stay, Waimea Plantation Cottages offers unique accommodations in restored plantation cottages. Located near Waimea Canyon and the Na Pali Coast, it's perfect for families who want to explore Kauai's breathtaking landscapes while staying in a comfortable, historical setting.

Hawaii's family-friendly hotels and resorts offer a perfect mix of relaxation, adventure, and cultural enrichment. From Oahu's Disney magic to Maui's nature-filled resorts, the Big Island's educational activities, and Kauai's serene escapes, these accommodations ensure that both kids and parents will have an unforgettable Hawaiian vacation.

# CHAPTER 10: HAWAII'S NIGHTLIFE AND ENTERTAINMENT

## Luau Shows and Live Performances in Hawaii

Attending a luau is one of the most iconic and immersive experiences for visitors to Hawaii, offering a vibrant blend of traditional Polynesian culture, music, dance, and food. Luaus and live performances showcase the rich history of Hawaii and other Polynesian islands, bringing legends to life through storytelling, hula dancing, fire-knife performances, and traditional Hawaiian feasts. Whether on the beaches of Waikiki, the lush landscapes of Maui, or the scenic shores of Kauai, luau shows provide a memorable, family-friendly way to experience Hawaii's cultural heritage.

1. **What to Expect at a Luau**

A luau is much more than a feast; it's a celebration of Polynesian culture that typically begins with a welcoming ceremony. Guests are greeted with a traditional Hawaiian lei, often made of flowers, shells, or kukui nuts, symbolizing love, friendship, and aloha. The night typically kicks off with cultural activities like lei making, Hawaiian games, or learning to hula. Once seated, guests can enjoy a buffet-style feast featuring traditional Hawaiian dishes like kalua pig, poke, poi, and lomi-lomi salmon, accompanied by tropical cocktails and drinks.

The highlight of the evening is the live entertainment, which usually includes performances from various Polynesian cultures such as Hawaiian, Tahitian, Samoan, and Maori. Hula dancers gracefully tell stories through their movements, while fire-knife dancers dazzle with breathtaking feats. The chanting and music, performed with traditional instruments like the ipu (gourd drum) and ukulele, enhance the cultural storytelling.

2. **Top Luaus in Hawaii**
Each island in Hawaii offers its own unique take on the traditional luau, and some are renowned for their grandeur and authenticity.

On Oahu, Germaine's Luau and the Chief's Luau are popular choices, offering beachfront settings and interactive experiences where guests learn more about Polynesian customs and traditions. Another standout on Oahu is the Paradise Cove Luau, which takes place in Ko Olina and is famous for its spectacular sunset views.

On Maui, Old Lahaina Luau is widely regarded as one of the most authentic luaus in Hawaii. It offers an intimate look at Hawaiian history and traditions, featuring a more traditional hula without fire dancing, as it focuses solely on Hawaiian culture. The Feast at Lele in Lahaina provides a more upscale and personalized dining experience alongside captivating performances.

Kauai is home to the Luau Kalamaku, one of the most elaborate luaus in Hawaii. It takes place at the historic Kilohana Plantation and features a theatrical production that tells the epic story of Polynesian voyagers who traveled to Hawaii.

On the Big Island, the Island Breeze Luau at the Courtyard King Kamehameha's Kona Beach Hotel is set on a sacred Hawaiian site and offers a mesmerizing fire-dancing finale alongside its cultural performances.

### 3. Cultural Significance
Luaus are a reflection of Hawaii's deep-rooted traditions, and attending one allows visitors to gain insight into the islands' history, values, and spirit of aloha. Originally, the luau was a gathering to mark important life events, such as births, weddings, or victories in battle. Over time, it evolved into the large celebratory feasts

that continue today, where food, storytelling, and dance are essential elements.

Luau shows and live performances are a must-see for anyone visiting Hawaii, offering a window into the islands' rich Polynesian heritage. Whether you're enjoying a beachfront luau in Oahu or an intimate cultural celebration in Maui, these shows provide an entertaining and educational experience that captures the spirit of Hawaii's people, history, and natural beauty.

## Night Markets and Cultural Festivals in Hawaii

Hawaii's night markets and cultural festivals offer a vibrant mix of local traditions, arts, crafts, music, and food, providing visitors with a unique way to experience the islands' rich culture. These events are a celebration of Hawaiian life, where the community gathers to enjoy food, music, and entertainment, all while supporting local artisans and businesses. Whether you're looking for handcrafted souvenirs, live entertainment, or simply a taste of authentic Hawaiian cuisine, Hawaii's night markets and festivals are perfect for experiencing the islands after dark.

## 1. Night Markets: A Feast for the Senses

Hawaii's night markets are bustling hubs of activity, featuring a wide range of local vendors selling everything from food to crafts, clothing, and jewelry. One of the most popular night markets is the Honolulu Night Market in Oahu's Kakaako district. Held once a month, it attracts locals and tourists alike with its lively atmosphere. Food trucks and stalls line the streets, offering an array of delicious eats like garlic shrimp, poke bowls, and Hawaiian barbecue. Alongside the food, local artisans sell handcrafted goods such as jewelry, artwork, and clothing, providing an excellent opportunity to pick up one-of-a-kind souvenirs. Live performances featuring local musicians and traditional Hawaiian dancers add to the festive vibe, making it a fun, family-friendly event.

Another notable night market is Hilo's Night Market on the Big Island, where the local community gathers in downtown Hilo to enjoy fresh produce, street food, and live entertainment. Visitors can sample Big Island specialties like malasadas (Hawaiian-style doughnuts), locally made jams, and fresh fruits, all while shopping for handmade crafts and souvenirs.

## 2. Cultural Festivals: Celebrating Hawaiian Heritage

Hawaii's cultural festivals are vibrant celebrations of the islands' rich history and diverse traditions. These festivals often focus on Hawaiian customs, music, dance, and food, giving visitors a deeper understanding of the local culture. One of the largest and most famous festivals is the Merrie Monarch Festival held annually in Hilo. This week-long event celebrates the ancient art of hula and Hawaiian culture through performances, parades, and craft fairs. The hula competition is the highlight, where the best hula dancers from across the islands showcase their skills in traditional and modern hula styles.

Another well-known event is the Aloha Festivals held on Oahu. Spanning several months, this festival celebrates Hawaiian music, dance, and history, featuring parades, concerts, and cultural demonstrations. The Royal Court Investiture Ceremony and Aloha Festivals Parade are among the most anticipated events, showcasing the pageantry of Hawaiian royalty and the spirit of aloha.

On Kauai, the Eo e Emalani i Alakai Festival commemorates Queen Emma's 1871 journey into the Alakai Swamp. This cultural festival is steeped in Hawaiian history and features performances, music, and re-enactments, allowing visitors to connect with Hawaii's royal past.

### 3. Community and Tradition

Night markets and cultural festivals are deeply rooted in the community. These events bring together locals and visitors to share in the islands' traditions, support local businesses, and celebrate the diverse influences that shape Hawaiian culture. They also provide a platform for small businesses and artisans to showcase their talents, creating a strong sense of community and economic support.

Hawaii's night markets and cultural festivals offer an immersive way to experience the islands' vibrant culture. From the lively energy of street markets in Honolulu and Hilo to the rich traditions celebrated at the Merrie Monarch Festival and Aloha Festivals, these events bring the essence of Hawaii to life. They are not only a feast for the senses but also a celebration of the islands' unique heritage, making them a must-experience for any visitor looking to truly understand the heart and soul of Hawaii.

# Bars, Nightclubs, and Beachfront Lounges in Hawaii

Hawaii's nightlife scene is as diverse and vibrant as the islands themselves. While Hawaii may be known for its serene beaches and lush landscapes, the islands also come alive after dark with an exciting mix of bars, nightclubs, and beachfront lounges that cater to a wide range of tastes. Whether you're seeking a laid-back evening with a tropical cocktail by the ocean, a lively nightclub with DJs spinning beats, or a local bar with live music, Hawaii's nightlife offers something for everyone.

1. **Bars: Craft Cocktails and Local Brews**
Hawaii is home to a thriving bar scene that features everything from elegant cocktail bars to laid-back tiki bars. One of the top spots on Oahu is Bar Leather Apron in downtown Honolulu. Known for its expertly crafted cocktails, this intimate bar offers a refined experience with a focus on unique and creative drinks made from

local ingredients, such as fresh fruits and Hawaiian spirits like Kōloa Rum.

For a more casual experience, visitors can check out Duke's Waikiki, a beachfront bar named after legendary surfer Duke Kahanamoku. Situated along Waikiki Beach, Duke's offers stunning sunset views, live music, and a relaxed atmosphere. The menu includes tropical cocktails like the famous Mai Tai, and local beers, perfect for enjoying while the ocean breeze rolls in.

On Maui, Monkeypod Kitchen in Wailea is another popular bar known for its craft cocktails and farm-to-table ethos. The bar features a large selection of locally sourced ingredients, artisanal spirits, and house-made syrups, as well as a variety of craft beers brewed in Hawaii.

**2. Nightclubs: Dance the Night Away**
While Hawaii may not be as famous for its club scene as larger cities, the islands still offer several energetic nightclubs for those looking to

dance the night away. In Honolulu, Sky Waikiki is one of the top nightlife spots. Perched on the 19th floor, this rooftop bar and nightclub offers panoramic views of Waikiki and the surrounding coastline. Sky Waikiki features live DJs, an outdoor dance floor, and a vibrant atmosphere, making it a must-visit for nightlife enthusiasts.

Another popular Honolulu nightclub is The District, which features a mix of hip-hop, EDM, and Top 40 hits. With a large dance floor, VIP sections, and a lineup of local and international DJs, The District offers a high-energy experience for those who enjoy a night of dancing and socializing.

### 3. Beachfront Lounges: Relax with a View

For a more relaxed evening, beachfront lounges provide the perfect setting to unwind with a drink while soaking in the beauty of Hawaii's coastal scenery. On the Big Island, Huggo's on the Rocks in Kona is a favorite among locals and tourists alike. Located right on the water, Huggo's offers live Hawaiian music, fire pits, and casual seating on the sand. It's an ideal spot to sip on a tropical cocktail while watching the sunset or enjoying live entertainment under the stars.

In Kauai, Lava Lava Beach Club in Kapaa is another great beachfront lounge where guests can kick back with a drink in hand while listening to the sound of the waves. With its "toes in the sand" ambiance, friendly service, and delicious menu of island-inspired cocktails, Lava Lava is perfect for a laid-back evening by the ocean.

Hawaii's nightlife scene is as multifaceted as the islands themselves. From sophisticated cocktail bars and beachfront lounges to lively nightclubs and local watering holes, there's a nightlife option for every mood and style. Whether you're looking for a quiet drink while watching the sunset, dancing under the stars, or enjoying live music with friends, Hawaii's bars, nightclubs, and lounges offer unforgettable experiences that make island nights just as exciting as the days.

## Stargazing on the Big Island

The Big Island of Hawaii offers one of the best stargazing experiences in the world, thanks to its unique geography, low light pollution, and the presence of Mauna Kea, a dormant volcano and the highest point in Hawaii. At 13,796 feet above sea level, Mauna Kea's summit is home to some of the most advanced astronomical observatories on the planet. With clear skies and minimal atmospheric interference, stargazing on the Big Island is a must-do for astronomy enthusiasts and casual observers alike.

### 1. Mauna Kea: The Stargazing Capital

Mauna Kea is renowned for offering a world-class stargazing experience. Its elevation, combined with the remote location of the Big Island, means that there is little to no light pollution, creating ideal conditions for viewing the night sky. The summit's dry, clear air and absence of clouds provide unparalleled visibility, making it one of the best places in the world to see stars, planets, and galaxies with the naked eye.

Visitors can embark on a stargazing adventure either by joining a guided tour or visiting the Mauna Kea Visitor Information Station (VIS), located at an elevation of about 9,200 feet. The station offers free nightly stargazing programs where knowledgeable guides use powerful telescopes to help you spot constellations, planets, and other celestial bodies. The VIS also provides information about the cultural significance of Mauna Kea to the Hawaiian people, who see the mountain as a sacred place.

For those looking for a deeper experience, organized stargazing tours often include a trip to the summit for a sunset view, followed by a descent to a lower elevation for nighttime stargazing. At the summit, you can see a brilliant panorama of stars, the Milky Way, and even distant galaxies.

## 2. Cultural Significance of Mauna Kea

While Mauna Kea is famous for its astronomical importance, it is also a deeply sacred place for Native Hawaiians. In Hawaiian tradition, Mauna Kea is considered the home of the gods and a place where the earth meets the heavens. Visitors are encouraged to respect the cultural importance of the mountain, learning about its significance through guided tours or by visiting cultural exhibitions at the Visitor Information Station.

## 3. Best Times for Stargazing

While stargazing on the Big Island is possible year-round, the best months are typically from October to April when the skies are clearest. The winter months are ideal for viewing the Milky Way and other distant galaxies, while during the summer, constellations like Orion and Scorpio are easily visible.

However, be aware that temperatures at Mauna Kea's summit can be frigid, even in Hawaii.

Visitors should dress warmly, as nighttime temperatures can dip below freezing, especially during winter.

**4. Other Stargazing Spots**
If you're unable to make it to Mauna Kea, there are several other excellent stargazing spots on the Big Island. Hapuna Beach State Recreation Area on the Kohala Coast and Ka'ū Desert in the southern part of the island are both well-known for their dark skies and excellent views of the stars. These locations offer a more accessible alternative for those who may not want to travel to the high elevations of Mauna Kea.

Stargazing on the Big Island is a truly magical experience, offering a glimpse into the vastness of the universe while connecting with the rich cultural heritage of Hawaii. Whether you're viewing the stars from the sacred heights of Mauna Kea or enjoying the night sky from a quiet beach, the experience is sure to be unforgettable. For those who love astronomy or simply want to marvel at the wonders of the night sky, the Big Island offers some of the best stargazing conditions in the world.

## Sunset Cruises and Dinner Cruises in Hawaii

Hawaii's breathtaking sunsets, where the sky is painted in hues of orange, pink, and purple, are best enjoyed from the water. Sunset and dinner cruises offer a magical way to experience these stunning views while sailing along the coasts of the islands. These cruises combine the natural beauty of Hawaii with excellent food, drinks, and live entertainment, making them a popular and memorable activity for visitors.

### 1. The Allure of Sunset Cruises

A sunset cruise is an unforgettable way to witness Hawaii's coastal beauty as day turns into night. Most cruises depart in the late afternoon or early evening, giving passengers time to enjoy panoramic views of the island's coastlines, marine life, and the open ocean. As the sun begins to set, the boat positions itself for optimal sunset viewing, often framed by dramatic landscapes such as volcanic peaks, lush greenery, or the Pacific horizon.

On many of these cruises, you might be lucky enough to spot dolphins or sea turtles swimming nearby, or even whales during the migration season from December to April. The calm waters and golden glow of the setting sun create a peaceful and romantic atmosphere, making sunset cruises a popular option for couples, honeymooners, or anyone seeking a serene ocean experience.

Cruises typically feature an open deck area where guests can relax with a drink in hand while soaking in the sights. Some vessels also provide live Hawaiian music, enhancing the experience with traditional melodies and the spirit of aloha.

## 2. Dinner Cruises: A Culinary and Scenic Experience

For those looking to combine sunset views with a gourmet meal, dinner cruises are an excellent option. These cruises take the sunset experience a step further by offering a multi-course dinner as you sail. The menu often includes local specialties such as fresh-caught fish, shrimp, teriyaki chicken, or even prime rib, alongside island-inspired sides like tropical salads, poke, and coconut rice. Dessert may feature popular Hawaiian treats like haupia (coconut pudding) or macadamia nut pie.

Some dinner cruises also include cocktails, featuring classic Hawaiian drinks like Mai Tais or Blue Hawaiis, as well as a selection of wine or beer. The setting, combined with exceptional cuisine, creates an elegant yet relaxed dining experience.

Live entertainment is often part of the dinner cruise experience as well. Many cruises feature performances of hula dancing, live ukulele music, or even traditional Hawaiian chants. This blend of culture and cuisine enhances the overall ambiance and provides guests with a true taste of Hawaiian hospitality.

3. **Top Islands for Sunset and Dinner Cruises**
While sunset and dinner cruises are available on all the Hawaiian islands, each offers its own unique perspective. On Oahu, Waikiki sunset cruises provide stunning views of Diamond Head and the city skyline. Maui is famous for its Lahaina harbor cruises, where you can enjoy the sunset against the backdrop of the West Maui Mountains. On the Big Island, cruises departing from Kona offer dramatic views of the volcanic coastline, while Kauai's sunset cruises along the Napali Coast are widely considered some of the most beautiful in Hawaii.

Sunset and dinner cruises in Hawaii offer a blend of relaxation, breathtaking natural beauty, and local culture. Whether you're celebrating a special occasion or simply wanting to unwind while watching the sun dip below the horizon, these cruises provide a truly unforgettable experience. With stunning views, delicious food, and the soothing sounds of the ocean, a sunset or dinner cruise is the perfect way to end any day in paradise.

# CHAPTER 11: PRACTICAL TRAVEL TIPS AND SAFETY

## Health and Safety in Hawaii: Ocean Safety and Sun Protection

Hawaii is a paradise known for its stunning beaches, crystal-clear waters, and abundant sunshine. While these natural elements create an idyllic vacation setting, they also present some potential health and safety challenges. Understanding ocean safety and proper sun protection is crucial for making the most of your time in Hawaii while staying safe and healthy.

**1. Ocean Safety: Respecting the Waters**
Hawaii's beaches and ocean are inviting, but the waters can be unpredictable. Strong currents, rip tides, waves, and changing weather conditions can make swimming or other ocean activities dangerous. Taking precautions and respecting

the ocean is key to enjoying Hawaii's beaches safely.

One of the most important tips is to always swim at lifeguarded beaches. Lifeguards can inform you about current ocean conditions, including warnings about strong rip currents, high surf, or jellyfish. Beaches such as Waikiki Beach in Oahu or Hapuna Beach on the Big Island have lifeguards on duty and post daily updates about ocean conditions.

If caught in a rip current, it's crucial to remain calm and avoid swimming directly against it. Instead, swim parallel to the shore until you are out of the current's grip, then swim toward the shore at an angle. Educating yourself about rip currents and ocean safety before you swim can make a big difference.

Additionally, be mindful of reef safety. Coral reefs in Hawaii are sharp and can cause serious injuries if stepped on. It's also important to remember that coral is a living organism, and stepping on or damaging reefs harms the environment. Wearing reef-safe footwear or avoiding areas with sharp coral is a smart precaution.

For those who enjoy water sports like surfing, snorkeling, or paddleboarding, it's important to be aware of your skill level and avoid hazardous conditions. Always use proper equipment, check the weather forecast, and follow local guidelines for ocean safety.

**2. Sun Protection: Guarding Against the Tropical Sun**

Hawaii's tropical climate means that the sun can be intense year-round, and sunburns happen quickly, especially for visitors unused to prolonged sun exposure. To protect yourself, use broad-spectrum sunscreen with an SPF of at least 30. Hawaii has also banned sunscreens containing certain chemicals (oxybenzone and octinoxate) that are harmful to coral reefs, so make sure to use reef-safe sunscreen.

Applying sunscreen at least 20 minutes before sun exposure and reapplying every two hours, especially after swimming, is essential. Don't forget often-missed areas like your ears, the back of your neck, and the tops of your feet. In addition to sunscreen, wearing protective clothing like hats, UV-blocking sunglasses, and long-sleeved swim shirts can provide additional protection.

The sun's UV rays are strongest between 10 a.m. and 4 p.m., so seeking shade during these hours or taking breaks from direct sun exposure is wise. Hydration is also crucial—carry plenty of water to avoid dehydration, which is common in warm, tropical climates.

Hawaii's beauty is captivating, but it comes with responsibilities to safeguard your health. Whether it's understanding the strength of the ocean or protecting yourself from the sun, being aware of potential risks ensures that your Hawaiian adventure is safe and enjoyable. By practicing ocean safety and sun protection, you can fully enjoy Hawaii's stunning beaches and natural wonders without any setbacks.

## Traveling Between Islands: Flights and Ferries in Hawaii

Hawaii is made up of six major islands open to visitors—Oahu, Maui, Kauai, the Big Island (Hawaii), Molokai, and Lanai. Each offers a unique experience, from the bustling streets of Honolulu on Oahu to the rugged beauty of the Napali Coast on Kauai. To explore more than one island during your trip, you'll need to travel between them. The most common way to do this is by taking inter-island flights, though there are also limited ferry options.

**1. Inter-Island Flights: Fast and Convenient**
Flights are the most efficient and popular way to travel between Hawaii's islands. The flight times are short, typically ranging between 20 to 50 minutes, and they offer scenic views of the

ocean and islands from above. The main airports for inter-island travel are Daniel K. Inouye International Airport (HNL) in Oahu, Kahului Airport (OGG) in Maui, Ellison Onizuka Kona International Airport (KOA) and Hilo International Airport (ITO) on the Big Island, Lihue Airport (LIH) in Kauai, and Lanai Airport (LNY) on Lanai.

The most commonly used airlines for inter-island travel are Hawaiian Airlines, Southwest Airlines, and Mokulele Airlines. Hawaiian Airlines, the largest, offers frequent daily flights between all major islands, often departing hourly, especially between the more popular routes like Oahu to Maui or Oahu to the Big Island. Southwest Airlines also operates inter-island routes and offers competitive prices, while Mokulele Airlines operates smaller planes, providing service to smaller airports and more remote islands like Molokai.

2. **Booking Flights**

Booking inter-island flights is typically straightforward and can be done online just like any other domestic flight. It's a good idea to book in advance, especially during peak tourist seasons like summer or winter holidays, when seats may fill up quickly. Prices for inter-island flights generally range from $70 to $150 per person, depending on the route and timing.

One of the great benefits of island-hopping by plane is that security procedures are quick and easy. Unlike mainland U.S. airports, Hawaii's inter-island terminals are often less crowded, with shorter security lines and more relaxed atmospheres. However, travelers should still aim to arrive at the airport at least 90 minutes before their flight.

### 3. Ferries: Limited but Scenic

While flights dominate inter-island travel, there is one ferry route that operates regularly. The Maui-Lanai Ferry offers service between Lahaina Harbor in Maui and Manele Harbor on Lanai. This ferry takes about 45 minutes each way and provides a scenic journey across the waters, offering a chance to spot dolphins, whales (during winter), and breathtaking views of both islands. The ferry is a great option for those visiting Lanai for a day trip from Maui or vice versa. However, ferry service is limited between islands, as there are no ferries connecting the four larger islands (Oahu, Maui, Kauai, and the Big Island).

There was once a ferry between Oahu and Maui, but it was discontinued due to environmental and financial reasons. Currently, for island-hopping between the larger islands, air travel remains the fastest and most convenient method.

4. **Island Hopping Tips**
   - **Plan ahead:** Decide how many islands you want to visit and book flights accordingly. It's possible to visit multiple islands within a week, but be mindful of travel time.

- **Pack light:** Airlines often have strict baggage policies, and carrying less will make inter-island transfers smoother.
- **Stay flexible:** Flight schedules may change due to weather, especially in winter. Always allow extra time between connections if you're planning back-to-back activities.

Whether you're flying between islands or taking a ferry, traveling around Hawaii offers an opportunity to experience the diverse landscapes and cultures of each island. Inter-island flights are quick and plentiful, making it easy to explore multiple islands in one trip. While ferry options are limited, they provide a unique and scenic way to travel between select islands. No matter how you choose to island-hop, Hawaii's natural beauty awaits you at every stop.

# Packing Tips: What to Bring for Your Hawaii Vacation

Packing for a Hawaii vacation can be both exciting and a bit challenging. With its tropical climate, laid-back vibe, and various outdoor activities, you'll want to make sure you bring the essentials while keeping your luggage light. Whether you're planning to explore the beaches, hike through volcanic landscapes, or enjoy city life, here are some essential packing tips to help you prepare for your trip to Hawaii.

1. **Clothing: Keep It Light and Comfortable**
Hawaii's warm, tropical climate means you should focus on lightweight, breathable clothing. Shorts, t-shirts, tank tops, and sundresses are perfect for most days. If you plan to visit higher elevations like Haleakalā or Mauna Kea, where temperatures can drop, pack a light jacket or sweater.

For the beach, bring a couple of swimsuits or board shorts, and consider a rash guard if you plan on spending extended time in the water or snorkeling. A sarong or cover-up is also useful for transitioning from beach to casual dining. Hawaii is generally informal, so there's no need for overly fancy outfits. However, if you plan on attending a nice dinner or a luau, a casual dress or aloha shirt will be perfect.

2. **Footwear: Stay Comfortable**
For footwear, pack a pair of comfortable flip-flops or sandals, as they are ideal for walking around town or heading to the beach. If you're planning to hike, make sure to bring sturdy hiking shoes or trail runners, as many of Hawaii's trails, such as those in Volcanoes National Park or along the Napali Coast, can be rugged and muddy. A pair of water shoes can also come in handy if you're exploring rocky beaches or waterfalls.

3. **Sun Protection: A Must-Have**

Hawaii's sun is strong, so sun protection is essential. Bring reef-safe sunscreen, as Hawaii has banned sunscreens containing harmful chemicals like oxybenzone and octinoxate to protect its coral reefs. A wide-brimmed hat and UV-blocking sunglasses are also necessary to shield yourself from the sun during outdoor activities.

### 4. Beach Essentials
In addition to swimwear, pack a beach towel or sand-free towel, which is lightweight and easy to carry. A reusable water bottle is key for staying hydrated in the sun. If you plan to snorkel, some visitors bring their own snorkeling gear, though many tour companies and beaches offer rentals.

### 5. Hiking and Adventure Gear
If you plan to hike, a small backpack will be useful for carrying water, snacks, and a light jacket. For waterfall or beach hikes, a waterproof dry bag will protect your phone and other essentials from getting wet. Don't forget a

camera or GoPro to capture Hawaii's stunning landscapes.

## 6. Health and Safety

While Hawaii is generally safe, it's a good idea to pack a first-aid kit with essentials like band-aids, antiseptic wipes, and any personal medications. A reusable face mask is also recommended, as some areas may still have mask mandates. Insect repellent is useful for avoiding bites, especially on jungle hikes or near waterfalls.

## 7. Miscellaneous Items

Other helpful items include a portable phone charger to keep your devices powered on long excursions and a guidebook or travel app to help navigate the islands. Reusable shopping bags are great for picking up souvenirs or groceries, as Hawaii encourages eco-friendly practices and bans plastic bags in many places.

Packing for Hawaii doesn't need to be overwhelming. By focusing on lightweight, comfortable clothing, sun protection, and the right gear for outdoor activities, you'll be ready for anything. Keep your luggage light, prioritize essentials, and you'll be set for a fun and relaxing vacation in paradise.

## Local Etiquette and Customs in Hawaii

Hawaii is not just a tropical paradise; it's a place rich in culture and history, with its own unique set of customs and traditions. As a visitor, showing respect for the local etiquette will enhance your experience and help you connect more deeply with the islands and their people. Understanding the aloha spirit, respect for nature, and sensitivity to Hawaiian cultural practices are key components of enjoying your trip responsibly and respectfully.

### 1. The Aloha Spirit

At the heart of Hawaiian culture is the aloha spirit—a concept that goes beyond a simple greeting. "Aloha" means more than just "hello" or "goodbye"; it also conveys love, respect, and a sense of community. When locals share aloha, they're expressing kindness and compassion. Visitors are encouraged to embrace this spirit in their interactions, showing patience, respect, and friendliness in return. Smile often, be polite, and treat everyone with kindness, from hotel staff to locals you meet at the beach or in shops.

## 2. Cultural Sensitivity

Hawaiian traditions and history are deeply rooted in the islands, and it's important to be mindful of this heritage. Respect sacred sites, such as temples (heiau) and historical landmarks. If you visit places like the Pu'uhonua o Honaunau National Historical Park on the Big Island or the Iolani Palace on Oahu, follow guidelines, speak softly, and avoid touching sacred objects. Show respect by observing the rules posted and listening to guides who explain the significance of these places.

When attending events like a luau or a hula performance, treat them as cultural experiences rather than tourist shows. Appreciate the deep cultural meanings behind the dances, music, and chants. Avoid disruptive behavior such as talking loudly or leaving in the middle of performances.

3. **Malama 'Aina: Caring for the Land**
Hawaiians have a strong connection to their land, embodied in the concept of malama 'aina, which means to care for and respect the land. As a visitor, you are expected to adopt this mindset. Always clean up after yourself, avoid littering, and respect wildlife. Don't take sand, rocks, or coral as souvenirs, as these are considered part of the sacred environment.

If you're hiking, stay on marked trails to avoid damaging fragile ecosystems, and be mindful of signs that indicate culturally sensitive areas. The islands are also striving for sustainable tourism, so consider eco-friendly practices like using reef-safe sunscreen and minimizing single-use plastics.

### 4. **Shoes and Personal Space**

It's customary in Hawaii to remove your shoes before entering someone's home as a sign of respect. Many vacation rentals and even some shops may ask you to follow this tradition. Look for a pile of shoes outside the door as an indicator of whether this practice is expected.

Hawaiians tend to be friendly, but they also value personal space. Avoid being overly familiar with strangers—especially by invading their space or assuming they're comfortable with physical contact like hugs, unless offered first.

### 5. **Language and Greetings**

Though English is widely spoken, you will hear a fair amount of Hawaiian language as well. Learning a few key Hawaiian words or phrases, like "mahalo" (thank you) and "aloha," can go a long way in showing respect for local culture. Hawaiian Pidgin, a creole language, is also common among locals, but visitors are advised not to attempt speaking it, as it's an integral part of local identity.

Respecting Hawaii's local etiquette and customs will not only enhance your experience but will also contribute to preserving the culture and environment for future generations. By embracing the aloha spirit, honoring the land and traditions, and being mindful of local practices, you'll enjoy a deeper, more authentic connection to the islands and the people who call Hawaii home.

## Emergency Contacts and Traveler Resources in Hawaii

When traveling to Hawaii, it's essential to be prepared for any unexpected situations, whether they involve health emergencies, natural disasters, or other unforeseen events. Familiarizing yourself with local emergency contacts and traveler resources will ensure a safe and enjoyable trip.

## 1. Emergency Contacts

In the case of emergencies, knowing the right contacts can make all the difference. For immediate assistance, dial 911, the universal emergency number in the United States, to reach police, fire, and medical services. Hawaii has well-equipped emergency response systems, and operators can assist in English, as well as other languages when needed.

If you require non-emergency medical assistance, each island has urgent care facilities and hospitals. Some well-known hospitals include Queens Medical Center in Honolulu, Maui Memorial Medical Center in Wailuku, and Hilo Medical Center on the Big Island. It's advisable to have travel insurance that covers medical expenses while abroad, as healthcare costs can add up quickly.

## 2. Local Police and Safety Resources

For non-emergency police assistance, you can contact the local police department. Here are some useful numbers for major islands:

- **Oahu:** Honolulu Police Department - (808) 529-3111
- **Maui:** Maui Police Department - (808) 244-6400
- **Kauai:** Kauai Police Department - (808) 241-1711
- **Big Island:** Hawaii Police Department - (808) 935-3311

Keep in mind that Hawaii is generally a safe destination, but it's still wise to practice common sense and situational awareness, especially in crowded tourist areas.

## 3. Traveler Resources

Several traveler resources can help make your visit smoother. The Hawaii Tourism Authority provides up-to-date information on attractions, events, and safety guidelines. Their website offers a wealth of resources for visitors, including current COVID-19 guidelines, road conditions, and travel tips.

Each island also has its own tourism board, such as the Maui Visitors Bureau and Kauai Visitors Bureau, which can help with local insights, maps, and brochures about the area. These organizations can guide you on where to find accommodations, dining options, and activities tailored to your interests.

### 4. Visitor Centers
Many islands have visitor centers that offer valuable information and resources. For example, the Kauai Visitor Center in Lihue and the Maui Visitor Center in Kahului provide maps, brochures, and local event schedules. Knowledgeable staff can assist you in planning your activities and answer any questions about local customs or regulations.

### 5. Local Apps and Websites
Consider downloading useful apps for navigation and local information. Google Maps

and Waze can help with driving directions, while AllTrails is excellent for finding hiking trails. The Hawaii 511 app provides real-time traffic and road condition updates, ensuring you're always informed during your travels.

Being prepared with emergency contacts and resources will give you peace of mind as you explore the beauty of Hawaii. Familiarize yourself with local emergency services, utilize traveler resources, and keep helpful apps on hand to navigate the islands with ease. By taking these precautions, you can focus on enjoying the stunning landscapes and rich culture that make Hawaii a remarkable destination.

# CONCLUSION: EMBRACE THE ALOHA SPIRIT IN YOUR HAWAIIAN ADVENTURE

As you conclude your journey through this Hawaii Travel Guide, it's essential to reflect on the extraordinary experiences that await you in this idyllic paradise. Hawaii is more than just a collection of beautiful islands; it embodies a unique blend of culture, nature, and adventure that captivates the hearts of those who visit. From the lush valleys of Kauai to the volcanic landscapes of the Big Island, each island offers its own distinctive charm and set of experiences.

**1. A Journey Through Diverse Landscapes and Cultures**

Your Hawaiian adventure will take you through a myriad of landscapes, each more breathtaking than the last. Picture yourself hiking the rugged trails of Waimea Canyon on Kauai, often dubbed the "Grand Canyon of the Pacific," with its colorful cliffs and cascading waterfalls. Or imagine standing atop Haleakalā at sunrise, watching the sky transform into a canvas of colors as the sun emerges from the horizon, illuminating the unique flora that thrives in this volcanic landscape.

Beyond the natural beauty, the islands are steeped in rich cultural traditions. Engage with the Polynesian Cultural Center on Oahu, where you can learn about the various Polynesian islands through authentic performances, crafts, and cultural displays. Savor traditional Hawaiian foods like poke and poi, and experience the festive atmosphere of a luau, where you can enjoy local cuisine, music, and hula dancing. Each experience offers a deeper understanding of the Hawaiian way of life and the importance of community, family, and respect for nature.

## 2. Connecting with the Aloha Spirit

Central to the Hawaiian experience is the Aloha Spirit, a way of life that emphasizes kindness, compassion, and respect. As you navigate your travels, embrace this ethos by treating the locals and their culture with reverence. Participate in local customs, follow sustainable tourism practices, and remember that every interaction is an opportunity to spread aloha. This spirit fosters a connection between visitors and residents, creating lasting memories that extend far beyond the duration of your stay.

3. **Planning for Your Adventure**

While planning your trip, remember to stay flexible. Weather conditions can change quickly, especially when you're exploring outdoor activities. Embrace the unpredictability and let it enhance your experience—whether that means finding a hidden waterfall after a rainstorm or enjoying a beach day under the sun. Pack wisely, prioritize essentials, and remain open to spontaneity.

4. **Health and Safety Considerations**

Always prioritize your health and safety while traveling. Familiarize yourself with local emergency contacts and traveler resources, and take the necessary precautions when engaging in outdoor activities. The islands are generally safe, but practicing common sense will ensure a worry-free experience. Remember to respect the natural environment, keeping it pristine for future generations to enjoy.

5. **Your Adventure Awaits**
In conclusion, Hawaii invites you to embark on a journey filled with unforgettable experiences, stunning vistas, and rich cultural connections. Whether you're lounging on the sun-kissed shores of Ka'anapali Beach, exploring the historical significance of Pearl Harbor, or hiking the breathtaking trails of Napali Coast, every moment spent in Hawaii promises adventure and discovery.

As you prepare for your trip, carry the essence of the Aloha Spirit with you. Leave with more than just souvenirs; bring home cherished memories, newfound friendships, and a deeper appreciation for the beauty of Hawaii and its people. Your Hawaiian adventure awaits, and it's time to embrace the islands with an open heart and a spirit of exploration. **Aloha!**

217 **HAWAII** TRAVEL **GUIDE 2025**

Printed in Great Britain
by Amazon